D0112570

WHO'S IN CHARGE?

WHO'S IN CHARGE?

Leadership Skills for Clergy and Others in Ministry

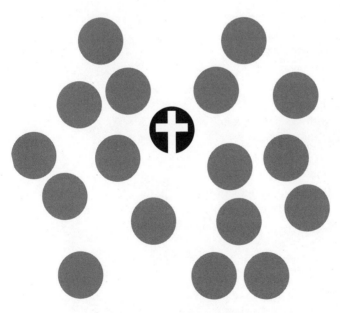

James E. Harvey

Loyola Press
Chicago

© 1996 James E. Harvey
Printed in the United States of America
All rights reserved

Loyola Press
3441 North Ashland Avenue
Chicago, Illinois 60657

Cover design by Frederick Falkenberg.
Cover art by Tammi Longsjo.
Interior design by Jill Mark Salyards.

This book is dedicated to Sister M. Theresa Margaret Yettick, S.S.M.O., whose skilled leadership and capable management of Maryville Nursing Home, Beaverton, Oregon, form an impressive example of the motto "Leadership, Not Drivership."

Contents

Illustrations

Preface

The dark blue letters on the buff background of a sign situated at the entrance of the Army Leaders' Course at Camp Roberts, California, proclaimed the kind of leadership the military wanted in the 1950s. The slogan read, *"Leadership, Not Drivership."*

World War II brought an immediate need to beat plowshares into swords. It also brought an urgent need to transform many of those who guided the plowshares into effective leaders.

Research by Army behavioral scientists developed significant data on the qualities found among successful leaders in military and civilian enterprises. Why is this research important? Good leadership creates an effective organization; poor leadership is destructive. The life and death of corporations, small businesses, military units, and governments depend upon good leadership. Good leadership is no accident.

The Army research team concluded that while some effective leaders have exceptional innate qualities, nevertheless, leadership is an art; *it can be learned and developed!* What they discovered in the 1950s still holds true at the end of the century.

Government and successful businesses and industries capitalize on what is known about leadership. The career paths of supervisors, managers, and chief executive officers bring an enriching exchange of ideas and methods.

Many problems encountered in the daily operations of the Church can be seen as a failure to follow well-established leadership principles or an inability to practice sound management procedures. Consequently, many tensions and difficulties within the Church need not exist.

By the very nature of their work, clergy are called to be leaders, yet this area of pastoral development is sadly absent from seminary programs. A job analysis of ecclesiastical functions and the skills required would clearly establish the crucial need for leadership and management training.

Many laypeople hold leadership positions in the Church along with the clergy. Some have come from outside agencies or businesses and bring with them leadership expertise. Others, however, have not had the opportunity for personal development in leadership skills. Leadership and management training for these people is important, too.

Who's in Charge? applies the principles of leadership, supervision, and management to everyday church operations. The examples and case histories are taken not only from church operations but also from government, business, and industry as well. In many cases, randomly assigned initials are used in the samples to protect the identities of those involved.

The wide range of managerial activities expected of a pastor in today's Church requires that many subjects be included, however briefly, in this book. Such cursory discussions of major topics cannot hope to be complete, of course, but they may suggest areas for further study.

Who's in Charge? will be helpful to both the experienced church leader who wants to incorporate personal experiences with opportunity for continued growth in leadership and managerial techniques and the seminarian who seeks to build on the foundation of others. It is also intended to be a useful guide for the nonordained church worker who is responsible for directing the activities of other employees and volunteers.

Acknowledgments

The use of selections from copyrighted material has been graciously granted by the following publishers and copyright holders.

"The Deming Way" by Mike Schmoker. Copyright © 1992. Used by permission of the author.

The Effective Executive by Peter F. Drucker. Copyright © 1966, 1967 by Peter F. Drucker. HarperCollins Publishers Inc. Used by permission.

Reprinted by permission of Warner Books/New York from *If It Ain't Broke . . . BREAK IT!* Copyright 1991 by Robert J. Kriegel.

It Doesn't Take a Hero by General H. Norman Schwarzkopf and Peter Petre. Copyright © 1992 by H. Norman Schwarzkopf. Used by permission of Bantam Books, a division of Bantam Doubleday Dell Publishing Group, Inc.

The Leadership Challenge by James M. Kouzes and Barry Z. Posner. Copyright © 1987. Jossey-Bass Publishers. Reprinted by permission of the publisher. World rights in the English language only.

Leadership Is an Art by Max DePree. Copyright © 1967 by Max DePree. Used by permission of Doubleday, a division of Bantam Doubleday Dell Publishing Group, Inc.

Leadership Jazz by Max DePree. Copyright © 1992 by Doubleday, a division of Bantam Doubleday Dell Publishing Group, Inc.

1

Leadership—The Person

We begin with the assumption that you are already a leader in church activities or that you will be, which leads us to a second assumption: because the Lord's work is involved, you want to do the best possible job as a leader. A third assumption leads us to conclude that you have had life experiences that form a foundation for your leadership. Experience has already convinced you of the need for some of the leadership qualities we will discuss. You may believe that particular qualities are obvious, but as we will see in our case histories, many church leaders fail because they have not incorporated these specific qualities into their leadership style.

What Is Leadership?

Leadership has been called the most important management challenge today. Business and administrative schools continue to conduct research in order to teach men and women how to become effective leaders. Such knowledge is important for anyone involved in a leadership role in service of the Church.

Leadership is not custodial care of a lifeless organization. Leadership involves actively and creatively presiding over a *living* organization in an ever-changing environment. The manner in which one presides is extremely important.

What, then, is this mysterious thing called leadership that allows some people to effectively unite the efforts of others in accomplishing goals while many would-be leaders fail? Leadership is the art of influencing the actions of others in such a way as to gain their respect, confidence, and loyal,

1

wholehearted cooperation in accomplishing an established goal. Leadership calls for special qualities in those who want to be effective leaders.

Sound leadership motivates subordinates, employees, or volunteers to perform well. It encourages them to use their talents and initiative and to develop their potential to attain their organization's goals. It is flexible. It meets changing organizational needs.

Drivership, on the other hand, is controlling and rigid. It strangles initiative. It is stagnating. It smothers the creativity of subordinates, employees, and volunteers alike. It limits their performance and growth.

Which of these two styles—leadership or drivership—work the best? In *Leadership Is an Art,* Max DePree describes the art of leadership as ". . . liberating people to do what is required of them in the most effective and humane way possible."[1]

Consider these case studies:

- Pastor A is bewildered by his continually declining church attendance in spite of his extensive efforts to be in charge of all major and minor activities. His volunteers eventually quit. His salaried help frequently leave when they are able to find other employment. Because they know how hard the pastor works, no one can find the words to tell him of the underlying cause of their dissatisfaction.

- Pastor B is in a neighboring parish. His congregation is growing. People often comment on the team spirit that permeates the parish's various activities. They especially like the excellent music that is offered and cannot help but comment on how much the music minister obviously enjoys her work. The pastor recognizes the talents of both salaried staff and volunteers and is careful to encourage their initiative and personal growth. People enjoy working for him.

Pastor B has the ability to liberate people for effective performance. Pastor A lacks that skill. Ultimately, the people in the congregation pay the price!

The newly arrived leader in any organization inherits an authority that keeps the organization operating. But employees and volunteers soon will be evaluating their new boss. It is a wise leader who realizes that one cannot rely on the temporary deference to authority to produce long-term results.

Research conducted by professors James M. Kouzes and Barry Z. Posner of Santa Clara University caused them to conclude that

> Followers determine whether someone possesses leadership qualities. Upper management cannot confer leadership on someone they select to manage a unit. Over time, those who would be followers will determine whether that person should be—and will be—recognized as a leader. Leadership is in the eye of the follower.[2]

The good news is that effective leadership can be learned. Business and management expert Peter Drucker underscores that point. "Effectiveness . . . is a habit; that is, a complex of practices. And practices can always be learned."[3]

We can begin looking at the complexity of leadership by breaking it into four categories, which we will discuss here and in chapters 2, 3, and 4: the person of the leader, the approach a leader takes to fill that role, rules of the leadership game, and the business of leadership.

The personal qualities or traits that leaders possess will have a definite impact upon those who work for them. They may not be able to identify or name those qualities, but they are decidedly influenced by them. Let's take a look at the qualities that are the hallmarks of an effective leader, remembering that they can be developed or improved by anyone who wants to enhance leadership performance.

The Traits of an Effective Leader

Appearance—A Matter of Image

The image a leader projects is perhaps the most important quality on our list. A positive image is the combination of a number of factors that help create a favorable impression. You have no doubt noticed the effort made by people running for public office to establish a positive image. Positive image is a combination of personal appearance, bearing, and conduct.

Clergy cannot neglect their image any more than can the president of a large corporation—that is, if they want to be successful. People who work for the Church may not have the finest clothes, but their clothes should fit well, be clean, and be in good repair. Personal cleanliness and neatness is a must. Good grooming is a significant factor in forming your image. In a busy world of parish life there may be a temptation to allow one's appearance to slide. Check yourself out in a mirror. Taking the time to have a favorable appearance is a requirement for the professional side of a leader's image.

The way you walk, stand, sit, and move can project an image of either confidence or a feeling of inferiority. Consider this simple advice on projecting a favorable image taken from *Life's Little Instruction Book* by H. Jackson Brown, Jr.: "Have good posture. Enter a room with purpose and confidence."[4]

Your behavior—on and off "duty"—will tell others much about their leader's character. Your demeanor does make a difference.

A favorable image is equally important for other leaders within the church organization—the director of religious education, the music minister, and committee heads, for example. Everyone in a position of leadership needs to project a positive image.

In summary, your image tells others what they may expect of you. It makes a statement about how you feel about yourself and your work. Your image, then, calls for careful analysis and a willingness to make improvements, if necessary.

Courage

Leaders in some lines of work clearly need to display the trait of courage. Commanders of fire, police, and military units, for example, must be willing to endure the same dangers as those whom they direct.

- Sergeant Ed Freeman commanded a police SWAT unit whose mission was to enter a building and arrest a man who had been firing a rifle at people in the street. The only way that Sergeant

Freeman could lead was by entering the building with his team. It was part of the job and was expected of an effective team leader.

There are times when a minister, rabbi, or priest will find themselves in a dangerous situation as well. Risks taken by military chaplains in battle are mirrored by other clergy who may be forced to confront an emotionally disturbed individual, a dangerous criminal, or a violent person. One's faith in God is a powerful resource in such cases.

But courage is called for in many less dramatic instances. You may have to correct a misguided volunteer. You may have to terminate an employee for misconduct or poor performance. Facing such unpleasant tasks calls for courage to meet one of the obligations of leadership.

- Pastor P. P. was a caring and sensitive man in charge of a large, active parish and school as well as a historic church and church grounds that were quite popular with visitors and tour groups. He used an accounting firm in another city because the firm's bookkeeper was the daughter of a former long-time employee. Although she was only a contracted bookkeeper, she functioned as an absentee business manager, approving or disapproving purchase requests and establishing her own financial policies and procedures. The operational and financial needs of parish, school, and historical site had to await her weekly visits. Frequent payroll errors were not corrected, and bills were often not paid on time. Employees complained that their requests for needed supplies were turned down or the quantities were arbitrarily reduced. It was painful for the pastor to end the services of the firm, which, of course, also meant the termination of the personal relationship as well. Finally, with increased pressure from the staff and the finance committee, he did what had to be done and established an efficient finance and purchasing operation "in house." The termination was very difficult for the pastor, but one that was clearly necessary.

In summary, to be an effective leader, you will need to have the courage to face unpleasant tasks and take appropriate action. It goes with the job!

Decisiveness

Decisiveness is the ability to make sound decisions promptly and then state them in a clear and concise manner. The decisive quality in leadership arises from your vision, anticipation of future events, and well thought-out goals. (The development of goals will be discussed in chapter 6.)

When you have clear vision of where your enterprise is headed in the future, many of your decisions can be made easily. It is the poor leader who has given little or no thought to the future who finds him- or herself unprepared and often caught up in someone else's agenda.

Naturally not all future events can be anticipated, and some decisions may have to be delayed until you have an opportunity to study possible solutions. You can minimize the number of such surprises, however, by your vision of the future.

The need for decisions will arise in minor as well as major matters. Your incoming mail, for example, will involve many minor decisions. Are you a compulsive reader?

- As a consequence of his many years in the ministry, Reverend J. E. was on numerous mailing lists. He discovered that more than 90 percent of his mail was unsolicited material. Reading each piece of mail could consume a significant amount of time each day. After quickly checking the return address to see if it might be an item of interest, he began discarding mail that did not have first-class postage. The time saved was used much more productively.

- Mrs. P. M. was hired as a secretary for a large parish. She discovered that the pastor, who had been processing his own mail, had boxes of unopened letters dating back three years. The letters contained donations, prayer requests, and other matters never acted upon. The decision-making process had become too burdensome, so it had been deferred!

- Mr. M. B., a business executive in a large corporation, advises making decisions promptly on most matters involving the daily mail. "There is a temptation to put off decisions on some minor matters 'until later,'" he said, "but the end result is a deep stack of paper which is not acted upon. Taking an extra moment or two to add a note and route the item to someone for action can improve your effectiveness."

Decisiveness does not involve making snap decisions. It involves making decisions that are based upon established vision, philosophy, and goals.

To help you work your way through difficult decisions, a decision-making process is discussed in chapter 2 in the section "Make Sound and Timely Decisions."

In summary, you will find that most decisions can be made with very little effort when you draw upon your vision, general philosophy, and goals. Unexpected developments can usually be put on hold while you complete the problem-solving process. While this process can lead to appropriate actions, some decisions will still be difficult to make. Even when decisions are tough, sound decisions will gain the respect of those you lead.

Dependability

For a leader dependability means the certainty of the proper and timely performance of one's work. As a leader you will be expected to do your best work, both by your superior and by your subordinates.

The quality of dependability is also furthered by a leader's vision, goals, and philosophy. Decisions are made that are consistent with past decisions, and this reliability strengthens the leader's relationship with those who follow.

Dependability builds a climate of trust that is so essential for good leadership. In the words of professors Kouzes and Posner, ". . . do what you say you are going to do. That may be as simple as getting to a meeting on time. It may be as difficult as not firing anyone during a downturn if you have declared you have a no-layoff policy."[5]

Some leaders fail in the dependability department because they are unwilling to limit their activities. They believe they must accommodate everyone. As a result, their performance is unpredictable. Here's an example of what can happen:

- Pastor M. P. was a kindly man who was reluctant to say "no" to almost any request. He often made verbal commitments without checking his calendar. He frequently committed himself to be in two or more places at the same time, causing delays and missed appointments. It also caused others in the organization frequently to drop their activities to fill in for him at a moment's notice.

In summary, effective leaders are dependable and consistent. You will want a good record of reliability. Those who follow you will know what to expect.

Enthusiasm

Enthusiasm is the display of sincere interest in the performance of one's work. The leader who does not enjoy his or her work will have difficulty in inspiring others to perform well. Enthusiasm is contagious!

The enthusiastic leader is one who constantly seeks new information about his or her field. After all, the Christian religion did not stop growing in self-understanding two thousand years ago. Subscriptions to quality religious journals and periodicals, for example, can build enthusiasm in a field that continues to discover new historical data and gain new insights into the inexhaustible riches of the faith.

How important is enthusiasm in influencing others?

• Dr. James Covert is a dynamic history professor at the University of Portland in Oregon. Each semester at registration time his classes fill up quickly. His reputation as a superb instructor is well known. Dr. Covert states that he became a history professor because as a child he listened to interesting discussions of history at his family's dinner table. He later discovered that many history teachers made the subject boring. Students were turned off. He resolved that he would teach history in a way that would make it come alive for his students. His natural talent was given a great boost by his enthusiasm.

Charles Schwab, a successful steel executive in the early 1920s, credited his ability to arouse enthusiasm among his employees to be his greatest asset.[6]

Professors Kouzes and Posner observe, ". . . it is essential that leaders inspire our confidence in the validity of the goal. Enthusiasm and excitement signal the leader's personal commitment to pursuing that dream. If a leader displays no passion for a cause, why should others?"[7]

In summary, you will succeed in inspiring top performance in others when you show your own enthusiasm.

Initiative

Initiative is the quality of seeing what needs to be done and then doing it.

A leader who waits to be told what is to be done either lacks initiative or has a boss who insists on making all of the decisions. Leaders who destroy the creativity of their staff deprive them of job satisfaction and seriously damage their own organization.

The competent leader not only uses initiative but also encourages others to do so. "The effect of enabling others to act is to make them feel strong, capable and committed," declare Kouzes and Posner. "Those in the organization who must produce the results feel a sense of ownership. They feel empowered, and when people feel empowered, they are more likely to use their energies to produce extraordinary results."[8]

- Officer Don Hochstein was assigned as a training instructor in a metropolitan police department. He was a highly creative teacher who frequently approached his supervisors with plans for new and improved training methods. His superiors recognized his talent and approved his plans. As a result, the entire agency benefited. He enthusiastically continued to use his initiative to devise new training programs for his department.

- Mr. C. D. was a part-time computer operator for a large parish in a busy community. When the pastor reorganized the business office and dropped an outside accounting firm, he placed C. D. in charge of all data processing. He was able to establish a number of cost-effective programs that were far better and less costly than those provided by the accounting firm.

In summary, as an effective leader, you should not only use initiative to accomplish your own work, you should also encourage capable subordinates to use their initiative. People who actively participate in their organization tend to enjoy their work more.

Integrity

Integrity is strength of character and soundness of moral principle, but it also includes the ability to be truthful and honest. The quality of integrity is essential for a leader, for it builds trust. When dishonesty, untruthfulness, or other forms of immoral behavior are attributed to a leader, the results are disastrous. As we have seen in our own time, the news media quickly sensationalize detected weaknesses in public figures. Church personalities are certainly not exempt.

Not only must the life of the leader be free of such defects; one must also take a clear and aggressive stand to promote virtues within the organization. Tremendous damage can be done in an organization by a leader who fails to take prompt and appropriate action against the immoral as well as the incompetent.

- The business manager of a large church activity was accused of sexual harassment by a female employee. Although the complaint was promptly investigated and verified by a member of the staff, the pastor delayed in taking appropriate disciplinary action. As a result, the employee retained an attorney and filed a law suit. The news media publicized the complaint, and the incident gained unnecessary and unfortunate notoriety.

There is a tendency in church circles to hope that embarrassing incidents will fade away. Some even hope that the responsible authority, by not taking action against the offending party, will be seen as a person of peace and understanding. As an effective leader, you cannot permit such compromise of standards.

Some years ago William G. Saltonstall, principal of Phillips Exeter Academy, made the following commentary in *This Week Magazine:*

Certainly many of us agree that the exercise of restraint is one of the marks of the good man. But in some areas compromise is flabby and dangerous. Any person of real conviction and strength must choose one side of the road or the other. It would be a strange kind of education that urged us to be "relatively" honest, "sometimes" just, "usually" tolerant, "for the most part" decent.[9]

In summary, as a leader, you must be a person whose personal conduct, behavior, and truthfulness are exemplary. You must also be recognized as one who will not condone inappropriate, immoral, or dishonest behavior by those for whom you are responsible.

Judgment

Judgment is the process of making sound decisions. Judgment involves weighing facts and possible solutions to arrive at a well thought-out course of action.

When a leader has the reputation of frequently making poor decisions, it is usually because of a failure to carefully gather facts and analyze their bearing on possible consequences. In other words, poor decisions are often the result of a failure to "look down the road" and visualize what would happen if each option were acted upon.

- Bishop M. N. often made decisions based on emotion, or what others called his "gut reaction." It was a good example of a failure to "look down the road." His decisions, often made in haste, were also at times explosive. He found it difficult to understand why his actions produced negative consequences. His failures were particularly evident in personnel matters and personal relations.

- Pastor M. P. learned from experience that his decisions often met with objections from other members of the staff who pointed out the likely unfavorable consequences. This troubled him, for he was eager to assert that he was in charge of the parish. As a result, he chose not to discuss any pending decisions. He became quiet and secretive before making major decisions. His staff was unable to help him.

Gathering opposing ideas can help you make better decisions. Management expert Peter Drucker advises, "The understanding that underlies the right decision grows out of the clash and conflict of divergent opinions and out of the serious consideration of competing alternatives."[10]

No one has a perfect record, but the leader who discovers that personal decisions are often faulty should follow the process recommended in "Making Sound and Timely Decisions" in chapter 2. If followed and poor decisions are still made, it is a signal for the leader to learn to consult with advisers. They may be staff members or experts in appropriate fields. If they offer divergent views, so much the better. In fact, truly effective leaders seek the participation of others in making decisions.

Many giants of business and industry have credited their success to their ability to gather around themselves people who were more capable than they were. Millionaire Andrew Carnegie credited those who helped build his success. The epitaph he prepared for his tombstone read, "Here lies one who knew how to get around him men who were cleverer than himself."[11]

You can use this same principle in selecting a staff, assistants, or helpers. Be on the lookout for creative people with a vision of the future. Then give them the freedom to use their talents.

In summary, as a leader, your record for making sound decisions will determine if others believe that your judgment can be trusted. Having good judgment is a significant aspect of your professional reputation that can be strengthened by your ability to enlist quality people to work on your team.

Knowledge

Two vastly different areas of knowledge are important for the leader: acquired knowledge (which includes one's professional background) and knowledge of the people one supervises.

Leaders usually are selected for their positions by proving they have acquired the knowledge necessary to perform their job well. But we live in an age in which new information emerges at an incredible rate. Professional people in our society find it necessary to attend workshops, lectures, seminars, and do professional reading to keep up on developments in their field. It is equally true of church professions that one can no longer run on yesterday's knowledge.

Because of the dramatic increase of knowledge in many professions, specialization has become essential. The church leader today may be either a specialist or a generalist, but there is an ever-present challenge to grow professionally.

The computer age gives ministry an effective tool that can be used for increased efficiency. Many leaders within the Church need to at least become familiar with what computers can do in the hands of a trained operator.

Developments in medicine bring new moral issues to be pondered, while Scripture studies in recent years give new insights on God's saving presence in the world. New concepts in liturgy, liturgical art, and music have emerged, making worship more relevant for people. Consequently, the church leader should be well-educated and stay in touch with current developments within and outside the Church.

Continuing education is not a luxury—it is essential for today's leader. You will need to make time in a busy schedule to allow for professional growth.

• Reverend J. C. was an associate pastor in a busy parish, but he made time to pursue his interests in computer science and music at a nearby community college. Not only did these courses broaden his background but also his interaction with younger students was intellectually stimulating. It provided an opportunity for students to discover that a clergyman is a genuine human being as well!

Apart from the acquired knowledge that is crucial to one's job performance, the leader needs to know the people in his or her working environment. The leader needs to know and care about them.

Certainly the church leader should be sensitive to those workers who are having severe difficulties in their lives. Family problems, illness, an unemployed spouse, or the loss of a loved one can affect one's concentration, level of energy, and overall performance. Knowing the burden a worker is carrying will help you deal with that person more effectively.

Knowing those who work for you also means knowing their strengths and weaknesses. It enables you to use their gifts more appropriately and more creatively. It enables you to assign the right task to the right person.

The opportunity to have contact with those who do the work is considered so important in some corporations that executives take special measures to be among them. It is an opportunity for communication. It is getting to know those who are closest to what we do.

Management experts remind us that ". . . sensitivity to others is a prerequisite for success in leadership. . . . So schedule some time daily just to get acquainted with [them]."[12]

- Mr. D. R. is the music minister in an active parish. Although the choir is large, he greets each person by name as they arrive for evening practice. He makes a special inquiry about members of the family and how they are getting along. Members enjoy being in his choir because his sensitive attitude is contagious, and they find themselves as part of a caring community.

You can demonstrate your knowledge of and caring about those working for you in many ways. A card to each person on his or her birthday assures them that they are remembered and important to you. Enter their birthdays on your appointment calendar. A wise boss will also remember Secretaries' Day each April.

In summary, as a modern leader you cannot rely only upon knowledge gained in the past. The role of leadership requires that the search for knowledge and truth continues as a lifelong effort. You will also want to know the people you lead and the small and large events that are important to them. Knowledge gives you the power to lead more effectively.

Loyalty

For the church leader, loyalty means faithfulness to God, to one's denomination, superior, religious community, congregation, country, local community, and subordinates. The need for loyalty in any enterprise is essential for its success. Consequently, it is an essential quality for the leader.

What may be surprising is the concept that a leader needs to be loyal to those who are followers. A leader should have genuine and continuing interest in their well-being. A leader should not only give moral support when they encounter difficulties but also have an active concern about their working and living conditions.

All too often it is the church worker who is poorly paid, has few, if any, fringe benefits, and is expected to work on holidays. It is ironic that some church officials who advocate "just wages for workers" pay their own employees so poorly. Their attention is focused upon someone else's turf. They are unaware of the hardships endured by their own staff.

- Mr. R. C. is the church sacristan and also functions as the plant maintenance worker. Because of his duties as sacristan he is expected to be on hand at all major and most minor church functions. As a maintenance man, he is also expected to work "normal" working hours. Consequently, on religious holidays he spends most of the day away from his family. He receives no compensatory time off—his daily presence is too important! He is often called in on days off and vacation days when a maintenance problem materializes at the church or school. His salary is well below that of others in the community who have similar duties and responsibilities.

- Mr. J. S. was hired as the business manager (or, as he preferred to say, "Chief Operations Officer" [C.O.O.]) of a large church activity. Eager to solidify his position with the pastor (whom he liked to call the "Chief Executive Officer" [C.E.O.]), J. S. recommended changing health plans to save money. The pastor agreed. The change meant that employees lost health insurance coverage for family members. In order to include a spouse and child under the new plan, an employee would need to have an extra $200 deducted from monthly take-home pay. In businesses where employees are represented by unions, such a change in benefits would result in a formal grievance.

No one was there to take the side of the employees at this church, however.

As a church leader, you will need to protect the benefits and working conditions of those for whom you are responsible. Loyalty toward the workers must not be forgotten.

Loyalty toward one's superiors means that you will support the goals and tasks you are given. If you disagree with the boss' policy, it would be appropriate to say so in a private discussion. But loyalty requires that disagreements not be discussed publicly.

In summary, as a leader your loyalty is required not only toward your supervisor but also for those whom you supervise.

Tact

Tact is the ability to deal with others without creating offense. It is a particularly vital quality for a leader. The importance of dealing tactfully with your boss may be obvious, but it is no less important in dealing with subordinates.

Leadership that "works," you will recall, is based upon gaining followers' loyal, wholehearted cooperation. So you can see how important it is to treat the follower—both employee and volunteer—with a large helping of respect. Tact is the lubricant that keeps human relations running smoothly.

Dale Carnegie's timeless work *How to Win Friends and Influence People* is an excellent book on human relations that has been a best-seller for decades. It should be read and reread by anyone who is serious about refining leadership skills. Carnegie emphasizes the importance of tact in dealing with others.[13]

- Bishop Y. M. is accustomed to receiving deference from others because of his position and title. Memos written to his clergy often include hostile words. Conferences, too, are salted with angry messages. One priest reported to his colleagues that the bishop "became livid" when he discussed a new compensation schedule for diocesan clergy. Unfortunately, the poor bishop is unaware that his lack of tact has an extremely negative effect upon his clergy.

The way in which a leader presents his or her observations is every bit as important as the actual words. Consider the following example of a tactful method of making corrections:

- Reverend E. S. is a chaplain in a city police department. Two employees work for him: a police officer and a secretary. At times it is necessary for him to correct their performance. E. S. likes to use the "sandwich technique." This technique involves recognizing specific instances of good performance of the employee before and after offering the correction. He tactfully "sandwiches" his suggested improvement between two positive "slices" of praise. The conference always ends on a positive note, and the employee looks forward to making the recommended improvement.

The language and the manner with which corrections are made are important elements of tact. The time and place for making corrections are also important. Whenever possible, corrections should be a private matter. "A leader ought never to embarrass followers," says business executive Max DePree.[14]

In summary, as a leader, tact will help your interpersonal relations to function smoothly. You will want to be as tactful in dealing with your employees and volunteers as you are with you boss. The "sandwich technique" is a useful tool for improving others' performance in a constructive, energizing way.

Unselfishness

For a leader, unselfishness means the avoidance of providing for one's own comfort and personal advancement at the expense of others. Father John Powell, the well-known Jesuit educator and author, states that when the happiness, security, and well-being of another means more to us than our own needs, we can truly say that we love that person.[15] Love entails a complete abandonment of selfishness.

From a leadership perspective, then, unselfishness means putting the happiness, security, and well-being of employees and volunteers ahead of your own self-interest.

Unselfishness is demonstrated by the practice of good military leaders who wait to eat until the last of their troops is fed; that is, assuring that there is enough food for others before taking their own meal.

Unselfishness for the church leader may involve the willingness to put aside one's own work or favorite activity to listen to the troubles of an employee or volunteer. It may mean offering to preside at a church function in order for a colleague to have some time off.

There is something fundamentally Christian about putting the well-being of others ahead of individual interests. Many opportunities arise in surprising circumstances. Effective leadership, though, requires balance. A forced effort to prove you are unselfish can interfere with your essential duties. Pastor M. P., the man who couldn't say "no," fell into this trap and disrupted his own schedule and those of others in the parish.

In summary, as a leader, you should be aware of the necessity of considering the well-being of those who follow you and placing their needs ahead of your own. You should remember their need for affirmation and generously give them credit for helping you accomplish your goals and objectives.

Personal Qualities of Leaders

Appearance–Professional Image
Courage
Decisiveness
Dependability
Enthusiasm
Initiative
Integrity
Judgment
Knowledge
Loyalty
Tact
Unselfishness

Fig. 1. Summary of personal qualities.

②

The Approach to Leadership

We have examined the person of a leader, looking at the qualities or traits that bring about effectiveness. We can work to improve any weak areas. Equally important, however, is the manner in which one approaches one's work. Effective leaders are guided in their leadership roles by a series of principles.

Know Your Job

Leaders who fail to grasp the major elements of their job will be unable to gain the respect of their followers. The person newly appointed to a leadership position may experience some uncertainties about a new role. Even an experienced leader who moves into a new position will need a period of adjustment.

Where do you start in order to know what your job entails?

A well-run organization will provide job descriptions for every position. They form the basis for agreement between worker and supervisor. Job descriptions are discussed in greater detail in chapter 8.

You should have a job description provided by the person to whom you are responsible. If no job description exists, you will find it helpful to create one based on your vision of the job. You can use it as the basis for a discussion with the person to whom you report. A bit of diplomacy is called for here. Explain that you want to clearly understand his or her expectations so that you can meet them. A mutually agreed upon job description can prevent needless uncertainty and possible conflict down the road.

- Newly ordained priests in a large diocese were placed in a three-year internship program. They were instructed to meet with their pastors and devise a "contract" that would spell out their expectations. This contract would be reviewed during the year and rewritten for the following years of the program. Such contracts are another form of a job description.

It is obvious that the job description of a director of religious education will be quite different from that of a music minister. What is not so obvious is that the job descriptions for clergy may be quite different, according to their assignments. Ordination does not bring an across-the-board expertise that prepares one for any and all assignments. A general, all-purpose job description will not do.

The demands of your job may change, or you may be reassigned. Either situation may call for new knowledge and skills. The principle of knowing your job can be most challenging.

In summary, as a leader you will be expected to know your job and be proficient in it. A written job description is an important guide in establishing what is expected of you. You will also need to have some understanding of the jobs of those who work for you, even if you lack the special skills to perform those jobs. Be alert for changes that may occur in the job you have been performing.

Know Yourself and Seek Improvement

Each of us brings together a unique combination of strengths and weaknesses. Effective leaders identify their weaknesses, and when possible, seek improvement. We have already noted that in today's rapidly developing world there is a need among professionals for continuing education. It is not just a matter of new information being discovered and new techniques being devised—the demands of your job may change.

- Pastor J. C. found himself in a parish with a changing ethnic composition. He took classes in Spanish at a nearby community college. He eventually attended a language school in Mexico to totally immerse himself in the language. This effort brought a dramatic improvement in his ability to minister to Spanish-speaking parishioners.

- Early in the computer age pastor T. W. saw the advantages of computerizing parish records and programs. He tutored himself in this newly emerging field. His fairly small parish benefited from his personal commitment to professional growth.

- Mr. J. H. is a lay minister interested in expanding his ministry to hospital work. He enrolled in a death and dying course at a local university to enable himself to deal more effectively with the terminally ill and their families.

Physical fitness is an area that most of us need to improve. Fortunately, we live in an age in which public attention has been focused on the necessity for maintaining proper diet and exercise. Unfortunately, those in a busy ministry may neglect them. But a correct diet and sufficient exercise are not luxuries. They are important components of a health maintenance program as are regular physical examinations to detect medical problems early on.

- Reverend T. O. regularly schedules the time to take a walk around his community. In this way not only does he maintain his exercise program he also enjoys healthy interactions with the people he encounters. It is an effective use of time, both physically and socially.

- Reverend H. J. believes that he would preach more effectively without using notes. He was concerned, however, with his poor memory. He worked to make his homilies reasonably brief and organized his main points in a logical sequence. He wrote them down, then prepared an outline of key words on a card to be carried in his pocket as an emergency reference in case of memory failure. As he gained increased confidence he stopped carrying the card. He developed the ability to speak to large congregations in a personal and direct way with excellent results.

In summary, as an effective leader you will want to identify your strengths and weaknesses—then find ways to improve them. It may be a matter of health, interpersonal relations, or some elements of your job performance. But the desire to always improve underlies good leadership.

Know Your Workers
and Look Out for Their Welfare

The president of a large manufacturing corporation will probably not know the names of every employee on the factory floor, but, even so, visits to the work area undoubtedly will make an impression. It will prove that their boss cares about them. The major general who commands an infantry division will not know the names of the troops in the mess hall, but they will be aware that "the old man" cares enough about them to eat the same food they have—and evaluate it.

While top leaders cannot know the names of all persons at the working level, certainly their immediate supervisor should. In the same way, the music minister of a parish should know the names and something about the people in the choir.

Knowing the employees and volunteers along with their strengths and weaknesses will enable you to appropriately assign them to new tasks and consider them for positions of increased responsibility. Unions play a key role in improving the working conditions of their members and assuring fair play. In the Church, however, employees and volunteers are usually not represented by any articulate, influential outside party. Consequently, the need for attention to workers' welfare clearly falls upon the leader.

- Recall our earlier case of Mr. J. S., the C.O.O. for a large church activity who arranged for a new health plan to save money. Consequently, employees lost health coverage for their family members. Without formal representation to protest actions that damage employees' working conditions and benefits, workers may be placed in a vulnerable position. Thus, the pastor must be deeply committed and sensitive to their needs.

- Bishop N. N. sent a lengthy memo to his clergy, promising them a salary increase in six months. He admitted that an increase was three years overdue. He concluded his memo by railing against using the consumer price index as a means of establishing the increased cost of living. His clergy noted that not only did they have to wait for an increase that was three years overdue, they would have to wait an additional six months to gain any salary increase. The bishop had no idea of the hard feelings his "generosity" engendered and the continued decline in the morale of his clergy.

A pastor who has associates living in the same rectory has a special obligation to consider their welfare and comfort. The old saying that the rectory is the pastor's house and that others are merely guests recognizes a rather informal perquisite seized upon by pastors. But make no mistake about it; it is contrary to the principles of good leadership. The leader is responsible for the well-being of those in subordinate positions.

- Reverend R. W. was the second associate pastor assigned to a parish church. He discovered that the pastor had two dogs that were not housebroken. They had the run of the rectory, which created a foul odor. The house cook was an indifferent woman with no understanding of a balanced diet. Her cooking was usually limited to fried foods. A pile of rat poison was on the floor next to the stove. Food had been placed in the refrigerator and forgotten. It decayed. Since the cook was also the housekeeper, the rectory was rarely cleaned. In the four years R. W. lived in the rectory, the windows in his room had been cleaned only once. R. W. left the ministry after finishing this assignment.

In some respects rectory living is like living in a military unit. One cannot pick where one lives or with whom one lives. Military commanders have learned, however, that the welfare of the troops requires that their quarters be clean and orderly and that healthy meals that are tastefully prepared be provided. Those involved in pastoral ministry deserve the same consideration.

Bishops have a clear responsibility to assure that when rectory living is required, the quarters are maintained in a satisfactory manner. Since a bishop has many other pressing duties, it is vitally important that pastors be selected with care. The practice of assigning a person as a pastor based on years of service alone does the Church a great disservice.

In summary, you will want to know well those people who work directly for you. You will need to be sensitive to their cares, concerns, and their financial needs. If you are responsible for the living conditions of others, you must provide clean, comfortable quarters and healthy, well-prepared meals. Your care and concern for staff members needs to permeate all levels of the organization.

Keep Your Workers Informed

An organization that does not keep its workers informed unnecessarily operates in the realm of mystery. Mystery gives way to rumor. Consequently, the competent leader keeps his or her people informed.

Some organizations publish a house journal, bulletin, or memo for employees. This works well, provided the information is published on a timely basis.

Staff meetings are an excellent way to disseminate information. Staff members immediately then carry information back to their departments. This method of distribution, however, is only as good as the communication skills of those who relay the message.

Keeping people informed helps build a team spirit. It lets others feel that they are "in the know." Team spirit is a sign of positive leadership.

In summary, you will want to keep staff informed about matters that affect them personally as well as matters that affect the organization as a whole. In so doing, you will eliminate the brushfires that are started by rumors and false information, and you will foster a feeling of teamwork in your organization.

Set the Example

The leader, by necessity, stands in the spotlight. If employees are expected to be at work on time, so must the leader. If employees are expected to maintain a neat and clean standard of appearance, so must the leader. "Do as I say, not as I do," is a saying that reflects an attitude that can cause trouble for a leader.

- Mrs. S. A. was an assistant to the Chief Operations Officer of a church activity and was responsible for gathering time cards. She criticized an employee for not having deducted an hour from his time card when he had taken time off for personal

for a position, the better are your selection opportunities. In some cases, you may decide to use an employment agency to benefit from their pool of potential applicants.

In many cases part of the selection process should include gathering character and work references. Be alert for unexplained gaps in an applicant's work history. Since some applicants will try to conceal parts of their past by falsifying dates of employment, a follow-up either in person or by letter is in order.

- A large church activity advertised for a business manager. The first applicant appeared to be extremely well qualified. He was interviewed by a parishioner who was a successful businessman, psychologist, and associate pastor. He explained some gaps in his work history by saying that he was hired to reorganize business offices that were in trouble and returned to school for graduate work as soon as he completed his mission. No follow-up was conducted, and he was hired. It was discovered later that he had concealed being discharged for improper conduct toward female employees and was accused of the same conduct on his new job.

At times you will not be able to select an employee or worker. They may have been selected by someone else and placed under your watch. An important part of staffing involves recognizing the individual's unique gifts and placing them so that these qualities can be maximized.[3] General H. Norman Schwarzkopf, the dynamic leader of coalition forces in the Persian Gulf War, recognized this principle early in his career. As a senior at West Point, Cadet Captain Schwarzkopf devised ways to involve all of the upperclassmen in running his student company. Notes Schwarzkopf, ". . . you have to figure out the people working for you and give each tasks that will take advantage of his strengths."[4] Clergy may have received a similar education, but appropriate assignments should take into account their personal talents and interests.

- Reverend J. E. was an assistant pastor in a parish for four years. He had developed his ministry to emphasize areas in which he had particular interest and experience: he established an art and environment committee, was active on the children's liturgy committee, and designed and produced worship aids for special liturgical events. Upon his transfer, he was replaced by Reverend S. N., who was assigned the same activities, unfortunately, without regard for S. N.'s unique talents.

The task of staffing can be summarized as putting the right person in the right job. It entails being flexible enough to capitalize on each person's positive and unique qualities.

Directing

Leaders get things done. They direct the activities of others. The manner of directing—the style with which the leader accomplishes this function—will vary considerably among capable leaders. Further, the level at which the leader operates will affect the complexity of directing. Some leaders want every direction placed in writing and rely heavily upon memos, instructions, policy statements, directives, orders, and the like. Other leaders are more informal, using personal influence and oral communication skills to get the job done.

Part of the function of direction involves the continuous task of making decisions. You will discover that even the most carefully prepared plan will have unforeseen developments. Just when things are going well, an unexpected increase in people wanting to participate in one of your programs causes a shortage of materials or available space. You planned to buy a new organ for the church, but the unexpected failure of the heating system puts that purchase on hold. Directing does not mean sitting back and letting a program or project run itself. It means being alert for changes and decisions that need to be made. It means acting upon those decisions—and getting the job done.

Coordinating

Effective leadership involves coordination. Coordination is the important function of interrelating the various parts of a program or project. But it also goes beyond the details of the project or program itself. It calls upon you to consider all of the people who might have a stake in your project or program and to gain their input and cooperation. It may mean making necessary arrangements with others who have some control over resources. It may also mean looking beyond your own sphere of action to see how the programs and projects of others may have some impact on your plans.

- The choir director is planning a program of Christmas music for the congregation and the community. He visits the school principal to be sure that the evening he has selected is not the same evening as the school Christmas program.

- The youth minister is planning a special program to attract young people and wants to arrange for a dynamic guest speaker. The speaker is available only on the Sunday evening that another parish group uses the meeting hall. The youth minister will coordinate with the group leader to work out a solution.

- The parish council at Saint Michael Church agreed to organize and operate a weekly bingo game. The pastor appointed a committee to study successful bingo programs and survey the neighborhood to learn which evening would not conflict with other games already scheduled.

A lack of coordination can cause confusion, wasted resources, inefficiency, and hard feelings. You will want to communicate with others so that your work will progress smoothly.

Reporting

Wise leaders keep people informed about plans, programs, and projects. They have a responsibility to keep their boss informed; it is also a courtesy to do so. It is embarrassing to not know what those working for you are doing. Remember to keep your superior informed about what is planned, what is taking place, and how things are progressing.

Wise leaders also keep others informed about plans, programs, and projects. It is important to let those working for you know how things are going, too, and that includes passing along praise and commendations. One worker commented that he had worked in an organization for five years and never heard about the good work he had done, but he sure heard when something went wrong.

Reports can be verbal, but many are in written form. A parish can print a weekly bulletin, the religious education director can send a monthly letter to the volunteer faculty (with a copy to the pastor), and the pastor can send a yearly report to the bishop.

Think of reporting up, down, and sideways. The more people who know what is happening in your organization, the better. An organization is alive when things are taking place. In turn, people like organizations that are alive.

Budgeting

A leader is responsible for fiscal planning, accounting, and control. The complexity of these functions will vary according to the leadership position. Bishops and pastors will need the help of professionals; those in other positions may not need assistance, but are nevertheless responsible for their unit's financial management.

Budgets cover a twelve-month period that usually will differ with the calendar year. This fiscal year may vary from organization to organization. There is no hard and fast rule that a fiscal year should run from July 1 until June 30, although this period is quite common. For the leader to do a proper job it is important that there be a clearly established budget planning process that allows ample time for the submission of budget requests.

A good guideline for budget preparation would be:

- Six months prior to the effective date of the new budget, alert all those who submit budget requests to begin their planning. This opportunity allows those who spend money to have input on next year's operations. It also offers an important sense of participation. Final submission of requests will be due in two months. The cost of each budget item should be included.

Four months prior to the effective date of the new budget, gather and organize the requests. Begin the decision-making process. The income and expenditures of last year and the current year will give an estimate of the new year's income and routine expenses.

Two months prior to the effective deadline, the new budget should be in finalized form. Unit leaders should have a final budget report showing what they will have to work with in the new fiscal year.

Financial experts often have some special form of budgeting process that they bring to an organization and for which they are well paid. Their program usually will be based on a particular budgeting philosophy. The program should also provide budget preparation manuals for all concerned and should include a standard form for unit leaders to use in submitting their requests. Some systems accept the activities of the current year as a base and only ask for a unit leader to justify any new activities or expenses. Other systems ask unit leaders to justify current expenditures, as well as new activities or expenses. And some systems ask what cuts would be made if the unit's budget was to be reduced by, say, 10 percent.

Some of these budget processes are very time-consuming and require considerable research. But the data gathered will assist those making decisions on the final budget.

Whether you are the leader of a large or a small organization, you are responsible for fiscal planning, accounting, and control. If you are the leader of a large organization with the assistance of professionals, you will still want to maintain overall control of the budget process. If you are the leader of a small unit in a larger organization, you will want to plan for the coming fiscal year, justify your plan thoroughly, and keep track of the results.

- A large parish hired an accounting firm to develop its budget preparation process and to hold monthly meetings with the finance committee. After a number of years the process was still in a state of uncertainty. Departments within the parish were not asked for their budget requests until sixty days before the new fiscal year. The accounting firm made the decisions about who got what, put it into computer print-out form, and delivered it to members of the finance committee the night before their final meeting. It was obvious that the accountants expected the committee to give rubber stamp approval. Most members had no time to review the work. But at least the assistant pastor did make the effort to cancel all appointments and review the proposed budget. He found that important items had been left out and that figures were not correctly tallied despite the appearance of being prepared by computer. A poor budget process almost caused disastrous consequences.

- A medium-size city had a complex budget process, but division managers within the different departments were given an approved budget for their division about a month before the new fiscal year. Division managers were also given monthly computerized reports on monies that had been charged to their accounts. While this seemed to offer a degree of managerial control, one manager complained that there was too much delay in the computerized reports. "When I order supplies, I have to consider that money has been spent. It may take three months for the city to finally pay the bill and have it show in the report. I keep my own records to keep from spending money I no longer have."

Moral: As a leader you must keep on top of budgeting matters.

Evaluating

How are things going? The leader needs to ask that question frequently. Are your programs accomplishing the goals you set? Are your projects on schedule and within their budget? Are your employees performing up to company standards?

Some evaluations are quite informal. You inspect the work being done and are either satisfied or dissatisfied. If the latter, a few changes probably need to be made. Evaluation has a clear connection with the task of directing. Evaluation enables the leader to make changes when and where they are needed.

On the other hand, some evaluations, such as personnel reports, are formal. A semiannual personnel evaluation system usually entails a written assessment of an employee's performance during an established rating period. Such systems are usually found in large organizations having many employees, and, while they may be used to identify people for promotion, they are most helpful as a basis for improving individual performance. This type of evaluation can be a useful personnel tool when it is properly implemented. Stores selling business forms and supplies may offer one or more types of stock personnel evaluation forms. Personnel evaluation forms are also available in computer software.

However, buying stock forms off the shelf and launching a personnel evaluation program without the preparation of employees or the evaluators can be dangerous. Employees may view it with suspicion and resentment.

- Mrs. E. M. was the office manager in a large parish. She supervised the work of two secretaries, one of whom was not performing well. After a number of conferences, the employee failed to show improvement. E. M. bought an evaluation form at a business supply store and intended to use it as documentation of substandard performance to terminate the employee. Since no formal evaluation program was in place in the parish, the pastor decided that the use of the form would be misunderstood, making it appear that the employee had been singled out for unusual attention. He concluded it was unnecessary. Memoranda of previous conferences would be sufficient to support termination.

Other kinds of formal evaluation exist. For example, there will be times when you want to verify that a contract has been fulfilled. A thorough inspection may need to be conducted before a contractor receives final payment. Or you may need to evaluate the quality of services people are providing before renewing their contracts.

- Pastor P. P. was pleased to see his church reach completion. The people had been waiting for this moment for many years. The contractor was paid, but it was later discovered that a number of electrical and plumbing problems had to be corrected at parish expense.

It should be clear that evaluation is an important part of the leader's job. Whether informal or formal, you need to know how things are going.

Counseling

What do you do when you discover that an employee or a volunteer working for you is not working up to the desired standard? As a leader, it is your responsibility to counsel that person in a positive and constructive way. In chapter 2 we discussed the need to ensure that your employees understand the tasks that are placed before them and the need to train them as a team. Your attitude in counseling workers who are performing poorly should be positive, as if you are sitting at a table next to them and examining the problem together. What can be done to help them?

DIRECTOR OF RELIGIOUS EDUCATION: "Ruth, I hear that your Scripture study class always begins late. I'm sure you know that's not fair to those students who are there on time. What can we do about it?"

RUTH: "My husband has been getting home late because of his business, and I can't leave the children alone."

DRE: "Would it be better for us to start class a half-hour later? Or . . ."

RUTH: "I think that would work. Or I might be able to get the girl next door to take care of them until George gets home. I'll talk to her. But let's move the starting time back. We'll probably get more students if we start later."

When you counsel a person about his or her performance—or about their conduct—you will want to make a written record. If the worker fails to meet the standards you have set and eventually needs to be discharged, a record of your counseling efforts will support that action.

Counseling is not always related to evaluating. If you have a warm relationship with those who work for you, you may find that they come to you for support and guidance. Psychological counseling is a professional field, and it is well to keep in mind that as leaders most of us are limited in our ability to deal with serious problems of this sort. Find out which professionals others have used successfully so that you can feel comfortable making a referral.

Instructing

Leaders may find themselves in a position where they are responsible for the instruction of others. In many cases the leader is an expert in his or her field and will personally offer the instruction. In other cases, the leader will arrange for the instruction of employees and volunteers by another person with the required background.

- Mrs. P. M. is the choir director in a large city parish. She is well qualified in the music field and instructs the choir members in such a way as to consistently gain their best performance.

- Reverend M. M. replaced an old, inadequate telephone system in a very large parish with a modern one. The new phone system provided modern features, such as call forwarding, voice mail, and speed dialing. Lacking a technical background, he arranged to have a staff member who understood electronics to oversee the installation of the equipment and instruct each employee on its proper use.

- Bishop M. D. recognized that many parish problems were in fact leadership problems. He arranged for a pair of experts to conduct a leadership workshop for pastors in the diocese.

Some leaders have the background to enable them to personally instruct those working for them. But, especially at the higher levels of leadership where one oversees a variety of specialized activities, instruction by the leader can often become impractical. Instruction, however, remains one of the leader's duties.

Leadership Tasks

Planning
Organizing
Staffing
Directing
Coordinating
Reporting
Budgeting
Evaluating
Counseling
Instructing

Fig. 4. Summary of leadership tasks.

⑤

A Few Words on Supervision

The term *leadership* applies to the directing of people at all levels. The president of a large manufacturing business is a leader. The vice president of manufacturing is a leader. The manager of a Sacramento plant is a leader as is the foreman of a group of workers in that plant.

The first level of leadership is usually called the supervisory or operational level. It is the lowest level where someone is responsible for directing the work of others, and in many respects, it is the most important. While the first-line supervisor may exercise all of the activities discussed in chapter 4, the tasks of instructing, evaluating, and counseling are probably the tools most frequently used.

Consequently, supervisors should be aware of these responsibilities and develop their skills appropriately. The music minister, for example, should not only be a competent musician but also an effective teacher. An office manager needs to be an adept evaluator and counselor as well as a good typist and receptionist. A leader at the operational level may want to develop skills in instructing, evaluating, and counseling to improve effectiveness. Classes at a local community college may also help.

While we speak of a supervisory level in organizations, it is also true that top management carries out supervisory functions. A danger lies at higher organizational levels, however. World War II General George S. Patton, Jr., warned that there is a tendency to "command too far down." He thought it best for commanders to direct the activities of the next lower level and to simply be aware of what was happening on subsequent levels.[1]

57

- Colonel Mel Pasta was the Deputy Chief of Staff for Intelligence at Sixth Army headquarters. During the day he would circulate around the office, observing activities. On one particular late afternoon he notified a department head about the conditions in his department. "She's had the same sheet of paper in her typewriter all day!" Pasta said about an employee. "That's not acceptable!"

Colonel Pasta's reaction was appropriate. He did not supervise too far down. He brought his observation to the person working directly for him, whose job it was to evaluate and counsel the nonproductive employee.

That brings up another point about supervision. As Colonel Don Richardson reminded his deputy commandant at a military school, "You've gotta supervise the supervisors." If you are in the higher levels of leadership, remember that you need to take the time to examine how people in your area of responsibility are actually performing under their immediate supervisors.

Many effective leaders spend time with people at the operating level for very positive reasons. It is one way of communicating the leader's belief that the work people are doing is important. It is also an opportunity for the leader and workers to get to know one another as individuals, which builds a bond of respect. And it is a way to learn how people doing the work believe that operations can be improved.

The pastor who takes time to visit a third grade religious education class sends an important signal about priorities. Of course, the other grades will be expecting a similar visit.

Many demands will be made on you. You will find the time to be present to your workers only if you make it a priority. We will talk about time management and make some suggestions about it in a later chapter.

The Responsibilities of a Supervisor

As a supervisor, your responsibilities lie in five directions and will call you to effectively fill five different roles:

1. A leader and trainer of those for whom you are responsible
2. An implementer of ideas—your own and those originated by your boss, staff specialists, and those people you supervise
3. A co-worker with other members of the supervisory group
4. A subordinate to your own boss and his superiors
5. A mediator of employee or volunteer needs[2]

These vastly different functions will require skill as well as a high level of interest and energy. In fact, everything that we have discussed about leadership thus far is incorporated in these functions. They offer an overview of where your energies should be directed.

Styles

People who study leadership and supervision often identify three styles used by people in authority:

1. *Autocratic.* The leader makes the decisions and demands obedience from the people he or she supervises.
2. *Democratic* (participative management). The leader discusses and consults, drawing ideas from those being supervised and allows them to participate in the decision-making process.
3. *Free rein* (laissez-faire). The leader acts as an information center and exercises minimum control. In other words, the leader depends upon the sense of responsibility and good judgment of those being supervised to get things done.[3]

These are arbitrary categories, of course. Leaders may move from one style of leadership to another in order to attain the best results. Which style is the best? That is hard to say. Your personality may make one style easier for you than others. Most management authorities today favor the participative management style, since it generates an enthusiasm and a sense of ownership among subordinates. The autocratic form may work well for some, but morale and a sense of noncontribution among workers may be a problem. While military commanders customarily use this form, the active participation of staff officers actually provides a combination of the participative management with the autocratic.[4] It is generally conceded that the free-rein style is the most difficult to use and the most likely to fail.

As you develop your leadership skills you will probably find it helpful to vary styles to meet new situations. An effective leader is flexible enough to adapt to changing conditions.

6

Managing for Results

You are interested in leadership because you care about the results that your work produces. If you are a pastor, you want your parish to be regarded as a well-managed, lively community of faith where effective programs operate. If you are a director of religious education, you want your programs to be successful, interesting, and well attended. If you supervise a group of volunteers who visit shut-ins, you want those to whom you minister to feel that they are still part of a vital faith community. If you are a youth minister, you want your programs to make a positive impact on the lives of young people. Everyone who wants to be effective as a leader is interested in results.

The work of the Church thrives upon the efforts of volunteers. "The more a nonprofit institution relies on volunteers, the more professional its management has to be," remarks a management expert.[1]

How can you get the best results from your leadership? By focusing energy, clarifying organizational ambiguities, and organizing paperwork.

Time Management

One way in which you can focus your energy more efficiently is by managing your time. Most people feel that they do not have enough time in a day to do all that needs to be done, or to do all that they want to do. Where does your time go? Here is a list of a few time bandits:[2]

- Telephone interruptions
- Visitors dropping in without appointments
- Inability to say "no"
- Meetings
- Involvement in routines and details that should be delegated
- Lack of objectives, priorities, and deadlines
- Failure to establish clear lines of responsibility and authority
- Cluttered desk, paperwork on "hold"

Management experts advise keeping a log for a week or two to discover how your day is really spent.[3] A record will eliminate the guesswork and enable you to gain control of the "time wasters." If you use a daily appointment calendar, a review of what you did for a few weeks may give you some insights about where the day went, but it will not show the time that was lost on things that are not on your calendar. That is why a time log will provide a more accurate indicator. Also, appointment calendars are often ". . . filled in accordance not with necessities . . . but rather with the will of the most energetic or bothersome person."[4]

Time logs will not only show you where your time goes. They will show you how much free time you have during the day. Executives customarily find that they have only one-and-a half or two hours of "discretionary time" at best, according to management expert Peter Drucker. Awareness of discretionary time will also underscore the need to effectively organize your schedule to save chunks of time for your own work.[5] This time can be extended by having calls and visitors screened.[6]

You will discover that a major culprit in the theft of time is interruptions. Some leaders solve this problem by arriving an hour before their office opens to have a block of uninterrupted work time. Others set aside an hour or more during the day during which they are not available for telephone calls or unscheduled visitors. Exceptions are made only for urgent matters. The door is closed. It is time to go to work!

The telephone is a major cause of interrupted work. Some leaders want to appear to be always available and insist on personally answering the telephone. But it is an inefficient use of time. A capable secretary who screens the boss' calls can make a great contribution. The secretary can say that the boss is busy at the moment and ask if he or she can help. Many calls can be routed to someone else who may have the best up-to-date information. When the boss does return calls, he or she will often have the answers to questions that the secretary has already looked up.[7]

- Reverend B. K. was an associate pastor in a large parish. The secretary worked directly for the pastor, only occasionally working for the two associates. He believed that in today's busy world that if every priest had a secretary, they would be much more productive.

- Bishop N. N. prided himself on answering his own telephone. He instructed the telephone operators to connect anyone who wanted to talk to him. Not only did he have a large number of unproductive conversations but also his own work suffered. Working long hours made him feel indispensable, but he could have worked more effectively during shorter, well-managed hours.[8]

What about the leader who has no secretary? How can the interruptions be minimized? The answering machine has become commonplace today. By blocking out a period for uninterrupted work, the leader can turn on the machine and still screen any incoming calls that may require urgent attention. By returning the routine calls at the end of the work session, the leader can also move the conversation along. "Fred, I have a stack of calls here, but I wanted to get back to you with the information you said you needed." The telephone will waste your time only if you permit it.

Closely related to telephone interruptions is the visitor who drops in without an appointment. Here again a professional secretary can avert many of these time bandits.[9] But it also pays to develop your own skills in controlling your time. If someone catches you in the hall or office and asks, "Have you got a minute?" an appropriate response may be, "Can it wait?

Can we talk about it later? I'm right in the middle of something just now." There's nothing wrong with letting people know that at the moment your time is not up for grabs.

We have mentioned that ineffective leaders often have difficulty saying "no." The more important your position, the more often people will want some of your valuable time. When you decide that you must say "no" to some requests—"Sorry, I'm not able to be there"—you may find that the person persists. Because of its value as a tool in dealing with overbearing, manipulative people, we will discuss assertiveness under its own heading. As an effective leader who controls time, you will need to be able to say "no" and make it stick.

Meetings are notorious for their capacity to steal time, but they are also a necessary evil.[10] Management experts advise that when meetings last longer that an hour, their productivity declines rapidly. Because meetings can be well managed, we will offer advice on running effective, time-controlled meetings in a separate chapter. But if you want to control your own time, control the time spent in meetings.

Saving blocks of time will enable you to focus on the task at hand and work more effectively. Reverend B. P. set aside one day a week as "desk day" and tackled the paper that had gathered there. We recommend making as many decisions as possible on paperwork when you first see it. Management experts estimate that you can make immediate decisions on about 80 percent of the material. Chances are you will not know much more about the subject a few days later, and you will have to reread each leftover item again to recall its content.

The accumulation of paperwork is such a common problem that we now have a yearly "National Clean Off Your Desk Day" each January. Thus, the stacked desk is another culprit in the theft of time. The search for a particular piece of paper can eat into the time you have so carefully protected. So dispose of paper as soon as possible. Management consultant R. Alec Mackenzie recommends developing the habit of "single handling"—making a decision, disposing of a letter or report, or taking the indicated action at the first opportunity.[11] Remember that you do not need to compulsively read junk mail.

If you do not have a secretary, set up your own filing system and use it. Competent secretaries usually are able to devise a workable system, but if you do not have one, you may want to seek professional advice. "A poor filing system is a constant irritation to staff people and a monumental time waster in terms of retrieving information," says MacKenzie.[12]

Delegating work to others is another way of freeing up time for major tasks.[13] Delegation is also an important element of time management. Some leaders impair their own effectiveness by holding to the old adage, "If you want something done right, do it yourself." Following that principle can rob you of time and also deprive another person of a valuable learning experience. Remember, as a leader you also want to help others grow and develop.

A lack of objectives, priorities, and deadlines can interfere with your use of time. Goals and objectives give direction and focus to your energies. A clear sense of direction will enable you to use time more efficiently.[14]

Not all business matters will be of equal importance. Leaders who are unable to establish priorities waste time on trivial items. Some executives refuse to have their "in box" on their desk in order to avoid the temptation of looking at each item as it comes in. Some incoming mail items will be important, others relatively unimportant. You may want to ask yourself what would happen if some of the unimportant items were not acted upon at all. As one time expert observed, "Refusing to do the unimportant is a requisite for success."[15] R. Alec MacKenzie calls this "the principle of calculated neglect" and strongly recommends its use.

Establishing deadlines will keep you on track. "George, see what you can find out, and give us a report at next week's meeting" is an example of the kind of verbal deadline that will keep the organization's work moving forward. In Mackenzie's words, "The imposition of due dates is mandatory for time management. When delegating a task or scheduling steps to be taken toward an objective—set deadlines."[16] You may set your own deadlines to be sure that your projects do not suffer from neglect. You will want to list deadlines in your appointment book, so that the deadline becomes a reality.

We have mentioned the need for an organization to have clear lines of authority and responsibility. Without that clarity, time is lost, for the organization operates in an atmosphere of uncertainty and confusion. Job descriptions and organizational charts are the means leaders use to describe authority, responsibility, and established channels. These subjects will be treated later. From the standpoint of time management, however, the lack of organizational clarity can be a time killer.

Assertiveness

Most people involved in ministry or other church work sincerely want to be responsive to the needs of others. This quality makes them vulnerable to manipulation. Some of our case histories demonstrate how a leader's effectiveness may be impaired by the inability to say "no." To be an effective leader you need to be able to determine when and where your energies will be focused. Time expert Mackenzie emphatically states, "One simply cannot achieve excellence of performance without concentrating effort on the critical areas. . . . Learn to say no."[17]

How can you, as a caring and sensitive person, find the strength of character to say "no" to what may seem to be a worthy request? First, you need to accept the fact that you are limited in what you can accomplish and must, for the sake of others, establish your priorities. Along with those priorities, you must set standards of performance for yourself.

• Reverend E. H. was newly assigned as an associate pastor in an active parish. He immediately was swamped with requests to be the chaplain of a number of parish groups. He determined that these commitments would require substantial amounts of time that could be better used in the service of a greater number of people. He made preaching his main priority, since by doing so he could influence hundreds of people on Sundays. His sermons, based upon that particular day's Scripture readings, were carefully researched and well prepared.

In the simplified case history above, you will find both the setting of a priority and a standard of performance. Following this approach, you establish a working philosophy of how to manage your time. You may have witnessed what happens when a person fails to set a standard for his or her own performance.

- Reverend R. D. was a kind pastor, but not well organized. He frequently was distracted by a variety of demands that were placed upon his time. Unlike Reverend E. H., he spent little time working on his homilies. One parishioner said that instead of calling the pastor's sermon a homily, it should be called, "Some random remarks by your pastor!"

The second step involved in protecting your time management plan is becoming aware of the ways in which others attempt to manipulate you. These well-intended folks probably do not think they are being manipulative. But over the years they have developed techniques to get their way, and they have worked! When you spot someone using a manipulative technique, with a little practice, it becomes easier to say "no."

How do others attempt to manipulate you? Therapist and sensitivity trainer Dr. Manuel J. Smith identifies several techniques: (1) an attempt to make you feel guilty because you "should" accept *their* rules, (2) an appeal to have you accept their sense of fairness, and (3) an effort to use "reason" and "logic" to persuade you to do what they want.[18]

You will know that you are being set up as the victim of a manipulation when your "no" is not accepted and when the other person persists in pushing his or her cause. It might go something like this:

PERSON: "We'd sure like to have you join our parish prayer group. We meet on Wednesday nights."

YOU: "I'm sorry, I'm not able to do that."

PERSON: (Looking rejected) "Why not? We really need you." (You should want to be there. Give me a reason that's more important than doing what I want you to do.)

YOU: (Falling into the trap) "It's a night I save for some things I usually do." (Feeling guilty.)

PERSON: (Looking somewhat righteous) "Why don't you save another night and join us? After all, it's only one night a week."

YOU: (Feeling like you've just been had) "Well, I suppose maybe I might, um . . . well, uh, let me check my schedule." (Gosh, that's my favorite TV night!)

What can you do when you realize that you are being led into a manipulative situation? How can you say "no" and make it stick? Dr. Smith says that the first thing to learn in being assertive is persistence. He suggests that you follow a technique that he calls the "broken record." To use this technique you would speak as if you were a broken record, repeating the point you have made, sticking to that point in the discussion, and ignoring all other issues.[19]

Let's take a look at the previous conversation and apply the broken record technique.

PERSON: "We'd sure like to have you join our parish prayer group. We meet on Wednesday nights."

YOU: "I'm sorry I'm not able to do that."

PERSON: (Looking rejected) "Why not? We really need you?" (You should want to be there. Give me a reason that's more important than doing what I want you to do.)

YOU: "I'm not able to do that."

PERSON: (Looking somewhat righteous) "Why don't you join us? After all it's only one night a week."

YOU: "Yes, it is only one night a week, but I'm not able to do that."

While such conversation at first may seem to violate the standards of polite conversation, it is a completely appropriate response to someone who has just launched an attack on your time management system. Once someone pursues a cause after being told politely "no," that person becomes an aggressor and deserves to be dealt with in terms he or she can understand. Your tone of voice should be calm as you assert your right to control your own activities.

As an effective leader you must be able to control your use of time and that will mean saying "no" occasionally. Do not feel that you always need to give reasons to justify your stand. You have the right to be the ultimate judge of how you use your own time. Assume full responsibility for it without feeling the need to offer any reasons or excuses. Adopting this point of view can help you avoid some unpleasant moments when a manipulator keeps asking "Why can't (don't) you . . . ?"

Additional assertive techniques are useful in dealing with aggressive people in other situations, such as a salesperson who persists in trying to sell you something you do not want.

Although we have limited our discussion to dealing with the usual time bandits, you may wish to do further reading or consider classes in assertiveness training.

Goals and Objectives

What do "mission statements," "vision statements," "goal statements," and "objective statements" have in common? Regardless of what they are called or the language that is used, they all are ways of directing our efforts to accomplish specific purposes. In this work, we refer to goals and objectives, but you may prefer other labels. In fact, even the words *goals* and *objectives* are used differently by respected authorities in the management field. The important thing to know is that your organization has a clear idea of what it wants to accomplish.

Why? Management authority George S. Odiorne says it quite clearly, ". . . management of our affairs on a continuing basis requires that we define objectives before we release energy or resources to achieve them. If you aren't clear where you are going then the road too must be unclear, and if you aim for nothing, that's what you will achieve."[20]

Consequently, you need to set both long-range and short-range goals for your organization. Long-range goals usually refer to goals you establish for more than one year, while short-range goals are those set for one year or less. The parish should have identifiable annual goals. Each operating unit within the parish should also have its own goals. For example, given a parish goal "to improve Sunday liturgies by the Advent season," the music director may want to establish related goals for the music department. One of the music director's goals might be "to increase the size of the 11 a.m. choir to sixty voices by September 1." At the same time, the liturgy committee may want "to improve the flow of Eucharistic ministers within the sanctuary at communion time by July 1."

Although "goals" and "objectives" are often used interchangeably, you will often find that objectives are used to describe actions taken to achieve a goal. Let's take the example of the music director:

GOAL: To increase the size of the 11 a.m. choir to sixty voices by September 1.

OBJECTIVE 1: To ask choir members to submit names of potential new members by April 30.

OBJECTIVE 2: To prepare an announcement for the Sunday bulletin asking interested parishioners to apply for the choir by April 30.

OBJECTIVE 3: To conduct auditions of new choir applicants on two evenings after April 30.

In the preceding case, the objectives are a means of checking progress in attaining the goal set by the music director. "Objectives must be specific, measurable, tangible, and under the effective control or influence of those setting the goals," declares Odiorne.[21] Notice also that times were established for accomplishing each objective. Sometimes these are called benchmarks, sometimes time lines. They are important because they allow us to measure progress in meeting objectives by establishing limits.

Goal statements, on the other hand, need to be written so that they clearly describe an intended outcome rather than merely the means for reaching that outcome.[22] They may be broad and abstract, but they need to be clearly written to remove any ambiguity. Goal statements should be as simple as possible.

The purpose behind setting goals, you will remember, is to allow you to focus your energies and resources for maximum effectiveness. You will not want to set too many short-range goals, or you will lose the advantage of that focus. Limit the number of goals you set, and work on the objectives that describe how you are to attain those goals.

Goals and objectives, because they do concentrate our energies and resources, can spell the difference between effective leadership and ineffective leadership. If you have established the goal of a new roof for your church this year and you are approached by a parish organization to sponsor a fund-raiser for some other cause, you are perfectly justified in saying, "I'm sorry. Our goal is to have a new roof for our church this year. It will be costly, so all of our fund raising is dedicated to that project. How about next year? Put it in writing, and we'll submit it to the parish council."

Effective leaders set goals and establish objectives. Goals are not secrets. They need to be articulated so others know the course that has been established and can do their own work more effectively.

Peter F. Drucker sums up the essence of effective leadership quite nicely. "The foundation of effective leadership is thinking through the organization's mission, defining it and establishing it, clearly and visibly. The leader sets the goals, sets the priorities, and sets and maintains the standards."[23]

7

Organizing the Organization

Effective leaders want their organizations to function well and that means structuring the organization to work efficiently. It also means eliminating organizational confusion. Many church organizations that started as small faith communities have not bothered to clarify organizational relationships as they developed. Lines of authority and responsibility tend to become blurred. Workers may find themselves in a confusing and conflicting web of demands from several people in supervisory roles, all under the impression that the workers are their own property.

An important management tool you can use to bring improved clarity to your enterprise is the organizational chart. What's so exciting about an organizational chart? Nothing. But it remains a valuable device for showing and clarifying relationships within the organization.

No formal set of standards exists for the construction of charts, so you may discover other methods of drawing them. What is proposed here is simply one way of diagramming relationships and their lines of authority and communication.[1] Using this method, the place in which lines leave and enter "boxes" say a lot about the relationship. The way in which lines are used is significant.

Organizational charts can bring improved clarity to your organization in a number of ways:

1. They can provide a comprehensive picture of the total organizational structure.
2. They can reveal organizational weaknesses such as:
   a) confused lines of authority or responsibility;

73

b) duplication of functions or authority;
c) a span of control that is too great;
d) a chain of command or chain of responsibility that is too long; and
e) inefficient allocation of personnel.
3. They can reveal organizational strengths.
4. They can provide a guide for planning.
5. They can form a basis for reorganization.

In addition, the organizational chart can be of great assistance when developing the budgeting process, particularly if you need to explain your organization to fiscal experts or consultants.

• Pastor P. M. accepted a parishioner's offer to fund a management study of his parish church, school, historical grounds, personnel, and financial operations. No organizational chart existed, even though many people were on the payroll. The associate pastor, who had management experience, suggested that an organizational chart be prepared to explain lines of responsibility and authority to the management consultants. He also saw this chart as an opportunity to clarify organizational relationships. He started by listing the names of people who were being paid by the accountant. The pastor was then asked who each person reported to—that is, who was that person's supervisor? Gradually a picture emerged showing the lines of responsibility within a large, complex operation.

Building a chart for a large operation can be time consuming, but it is well worth the effort. Smaller organizations can also benefit. The chart can assure that everyone understands their place in the enterprise and the proper channels of communication.

Because they are a visual representation of an organization, charts can only tell part of the story. They should be supplemented by written job descriptions, directives, and statements of goals and objectives. But the visual story told by an organizational chart can offer a clarity that would otherwise be lost using words only.

We begin with a few principles of chart construction.

1. The chart should be well designed with its purpose always of paramount importance. While symmetry is desirable, it must not become the objective.
2. Keep the chart simple; it may not be possible to show everything on one chart.
3. The legend should be easy to interpret.
4. Charts should be up-to-date.

An organization can be put together in various ways. *Functional* or *geographic* types of organization may be utilized at the diocesan level with a few variations in charting techniques. Briefly, a functional organization provides special services to a number of suborganizations. A family life office, for example, may provide support services to every parish in the diocese. The diocese is also organized in geographic areas, such as parishes.

Two common types of organizations, the *line* and *line and staff* types, are most suitable for church groups. Line is a basic type of organization in which each subordinate is responsible to only one superior. A line type may not exist in pure form within an organization, but it may be combined with other types of organization, such as, line and staff or functional organizations. At least part of the organization will likely have a pure line arrangement. Direct line authority is shown by a solid line from the middle of the bottom of the "superior's" box to the middle of the top of the "subordinate's" box. Thus, a line organization looks like the following:

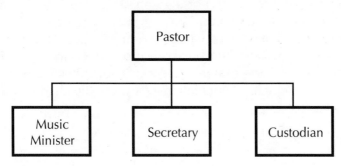

Fig. 5. Line organization.

Of course, few organizations are that simple. The leader of an organization usually will have people who help run the enterprise but are not in the chain of command or responsibility. Although not leadership roles, the work of these staff people is important. Staff positions can be indicated on charts by the absence of a line of authority from the staff box to other or lower level positions. The line to the staff position enters the staff box at the side, from the bottom of the superior's box if the work is done primarily for that person, or, from the command line if staff work is done for the organization as a whole. A line and staff organization looks like the following:

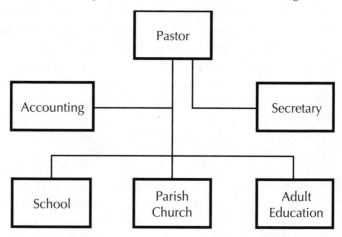

Fig. 6. A Line and staff organization. In this example the secretary works for the pastor, while accounting serves the entire organization.

Notice in this organizational chart that a box may indicate either a person (secretary) or a group of persons in a suborganization, such as a school.

If an organization is very large it is more practical for suborganizations to show their breakdown on a separate chart. The school in the above example might be shown that way for the pastor, but the school principal may arrange the chart a bit differently:

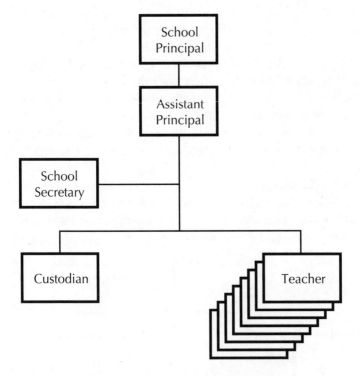

Fig. 7. A Line and staff organization in which directives usually pass through an assistant.

In the above example, the principal has given the assistant principal direct authority over the teachers and the custodian. Naturally there will be times when the principal will wish to deal with those people directly. You could add a second line from the principal's box to the line connecting the custodian and the teachers, but this would only be confusing. It is best to omit it. People generally listen to the person in charge without having to show it on a chart. Depending upon the relationship between principal and assistant principal, it may be a better organizational practice to show the person in a staff position with the position itself off to the side of the command line.

Notice, too, the way in which the teacher boxes are stacked. When an organization's positions are identical, it is common practice to show them in a stack with the number of boxes equal to the number of positions. But this method may not suit the needs of the principal who may want to spread the boxes out and put names and grades in them. That's fine, too. Remember organizational charts are meant to be aids that people can adapt as they see fit.

Thus far the examples we have examined show levels of authority. The charts are drawn from the top–down rather than depicting diminishing authority from left to right or some other arrangement. Levels of authority from the top–down are more easily understood. Anyone reading the chart expects to see the person at "the top" of the organization to be at the top of the chart.

One additional device is used in showing relationships. Committees and other consultatory groups are often a part of organizational life, and they should also appear on the charts. An example of charting this kind of relationship is given in figure 8.

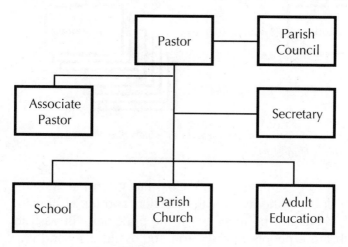

Fig. 8. The parish council is shown as an advisory group for the pastor.

What about the associate pastor in the above illustration? In order to follow the principle that people should be responsible to only one person, the associate pastor is shown as having no direct authority in the organization. Informally, he might be considered the "eyes and ears" of the pastor, but, in reality, this is no real authority at all. He might have responsibilities assigned to him by written directives, for example, to be responsible for personnel, payroll, and liturgical matters. He might have been placed on the chart in the same way the assistant principal was shown in figure 7. Or the pastor might have elected to give him authority over the educational programs, in which case the organization would take on a different configuration:

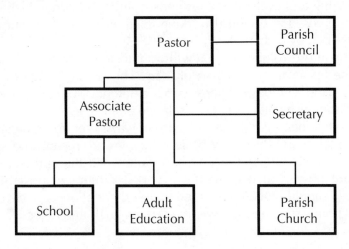

Fig. 9. The associate pastor has direct authority over the education programs and reports directly to the pastor.

Line and staff organizations are capable of further combinations. For example, a staff function may be organized internally as a line organization. It would be charted as so:

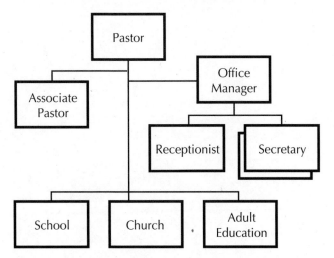

Fig. 10. The office manager is a staff position, but the office internally is a line type organization.

Even though some persons in our examples may work for a number of people, they should have only one boss. That is, there should be only one supervisor who is responsible for directing and evaluating their performance. Written guidelines may be used to establish working relationships that cannot be described by a chart alone.

If you use volunteers, you will want to show them, too. They make up an important part of many church organizations. A box made with dashed lines or in a different color can be used to distinguish volunteers from salaried employees.

Remember, there is no one correct way to set up an organizational chart. These few basic principles are meant to assist you in their preparation. A chart cannot tell the entire story about how your organization works. Whenever possible, charts should be complimented by job descriptions, directives, and policy statements, as well as written goals and objectives.

⑧

Managing the Paper

As a leader, you will probably have to deal with a lot of paperwork. The amount and extent of your involvement will depend upon the kind of position you hold and where you fit into the organization.

As we have already mentioned, much of the mail you receive will be junk mail and should be quickly disposed of. Some mail will need your attention, and some you will give to others for action, information, or filing. Clearly, you need to have a system to handle the flow of paper.

Routing Documents

Normally your paperwork will arrive at the business office of your organization. How this office is laid out is an organizational challenge all its own. A receptionist or secretary usually will receive the mail and other incoming paperwork or messages. What happens next is a procedural matter determined by the boss. It is a sound management practice to have the paperwork procedure written down. While a long-time office worker may know which mail to open and route to others and which mail to send along unopened to the addressee, a substitute worker may not. Having a written procedure also forces the boss to be clear on how paper is to flow within the organization.

Some documents will be circulated for the information and comments of others. How does your system control the flow of such paper to assure that those who should have access to specific items actually receive them? Some offices use a "Memo Routing Slip" that is stapled to the document, and others use a

"Routing Stamp" to place an inked impression on the first page. Both are used in the same way; the routing of the document is indicated—often by numbers to designate the sequence of persons to see the document, along with a place for their initials and date. Two typical examples are given in figure 11.

ROUTING		
To	Initl	Date
Pastor		
Asst. Pastor		
Business Off.		
School		
Religious Ed.		
Music Minister		
Home Ministries		
Secretary/file		

ROUTING		
To	Initl	Date
Pastor		
Assoc. Pastors		
Office Manager		
Accounting		
School		
Liturgy Dept.		
Ministerial Svc.		
Office file		

☐ Information   ☐ Action
☐ Provide Info   ☐ Comment
☐ Recommend   ☐ See me

Originator:

Fig. 11. Two typical devices for controlling the flow of paper. The routing stamp is shown on the left; the routing slip on the right.

Tips on Correspondence

If you are a leader who is responsible for correspondence leaving your office, you are also responsible for the quality of that work. Hopefully, you will have a competent secretary who is able to prepare neat, error-free letters and memos. But when you sign your name to correspondence, you imply that document meets your standards. You should proofread all the documents that you sign. Be sure they are dated. The failure to proofread documents can lead to embarrassing incidents, and, in the worst possible scenario, may end up in court.

We tend to become used to things as they are and not detect deficiencies. While it seems obvious that every organization should have the company address on their letterhead, one well-established church had been using stationery for many years with a nice logo, but no return address. We recommend that you check your letterhead. It is a sound business practice to include the address, telephone number, and fax number on letterheads to facilitate communication. It is also a good practice to include your organization's telephone number on company checks—just in case someone attempts to pass a check that has been stolen.

Interoffice Memos

Interoffice memos are commonly used to communicate within an organization. While they follow a different format from regular correspondence, it is appropriate to publish them on a letterhead or a special form so that the organization itself is identified. The order of the sequences may vary. We prefer the "subject—to—date" sequence. Once the document arrives at its intended destination, it will be filed according to its subject. It is helpful, then, to have the subject located where it can be easily read. Some organizations include "from" in the heading. We have placed it at the end of our interoffice memo example. In this way, it indicates that the memo is complete and that no additional pages exist.

St. Mary Star of the Sea Parish
P.O. Box 265
Warrenton, OR 97146
(503) 355-2100

MEMORANDUM

SUBJECT: Submission of Budget Requests
TO: Department Heads
DATE: March 15, 1994

The Parish Finance Committee will begin work on the budget for fiscal year 1995 in the near future. Please submit your budget requests to me by April 15, 1994. Follow the same format that we used last year.

Rev. Ted Weber
Pastor

Fig. 12. A type of interoffice memorandum.

Memos can be used for a variety of administrative purposes. Specialized functions should be clearly identified. Memos dealing with personnel issues can be titled "Personnel Memo" or "Personnel Action" and should be designated with a file number. The use of a file number is an effective way to refer to the memo later:

Personnel Memo 94–3 referring to the appointment of Linda Best as data entry clerk is amended to read "effective February 7, 1994."

A convenient numbering system can combine the last two numbers of the current year and a serial numbering of that particular type of memo.

Policy Statements

The memo format, slightly modified, can also be used for publishing policy statements. When a leader's policy is published it enables others to handle matters that would otherwise have to be routed back to the leader for a decision. It is another method used by effective leaders to manage their time wisely, for it enables action to be taken at the lowest possible level.

A policy statement should identify the organization involved —usually it is written on a letterhead. It should be dated, the subject should be given in the heading, and it should be signed by the policymaker. We recommend two main headings: policy and background. The statement of the policy should be as brief and clear as possible. The policy section is where people will find the answer to the question, "What is the policy on . . . ?" The background section can give the history and rationale behind the policy as well as cite relevant laws and regulations. Often this section can be brief, too.

• A priest complained that his diocesan confirmation policy consisted of four pages of ponderous rambling that had the policy buried deep within it. Whenever someone asked a question about the policy, he had to wade through the document to get the answers.

We have taken this policy and adapted it to the format that we recommend. We also eliminated most of the background material that did not directly contribute to the policy.

Diocese of XYZ
2132 West Bishop's Drive
San Simeon, CA 93452

POLICY STATEMENT

July 1, 1994
SUBJECT: Confirmation Requirements

POLICY:
Effective September 1, 1995, students will ordinarily receive the Sacrament of Confirmation when they are in the ninth or tenth grade.

For special pastoral reasons, exceptions may be allowed for the Confirmation of those in younger grades, but permission must be requested from the bishop before the program begins.

Students attending Catholic high schools are to be involved in the parish Confirmation program on a regular basis.

It is recommended that preparation for the sacrament should be extended over a two-year period.

Parents and sponsors should be provided an informational program. As a bare minimum they should be advised by mail of an overview of the Confirmation program and their responsibilities.

While involvement of one or both parents in the preparation program is greatly encouraged, their failure to do so will not cause an otherwise qualified candidate to be dismissed from the program; to deny or even defer the reception of the sacrament.

BACKGROUND:
The Pastoral Research and Practices Committee of the National Conference of Catholic Bishops conducted several studies on the age of young people at Confirmation throughout the United States. The practices were found to be so divergent that the Conference decided to let the matter be determined by the diocesan bishop for his own jurisdiction. The present policy emphasizes the Sacrament of Confirmation as a sacrament of Christian maturity and commitment.

Most Reverend John B. Brief
Bishop XYZ

Fig. 13. The format of a policy statement.

While this policy statement contains ambiguities that are best avoided, such as the words *recommended* and *should,* we retained the language of the original four-page document to the greatest extent possible. Although not an ideal model of a policy statement, it does show how a policy can be written in a manner that allows the reader to quickly determine the essential content.

Policy statements should cover a single subject. A pastor might have separate policy statements on such topics as marriages of nonparishioners, use of the church for weddings, use of the parish hall by parish groups, and the after-hours use of school or other parish facilities.

Job Descriptions

Job descriptions are an important management tool, yet many church organizations neglect them. If job descriptions do not already exist in your organization, now is the time to establish them. To create new job descriptions, supervisors should confer with their subordinates to determine their duties. The description then becomes an agreement between the worker and the supervisor about job expectations. Job descriptions are not set in concrete, however. They should be reviewed periodically.

Has the job changed since the description was last written? Again, here is another opportunity for the supervisor and the worker to sit down together and discuss the job.

The time will come when a position becomes vacant. An announcement of the search for a qualified person to fill the job must then be prepared. The central part of the announcement will be the job description. Of course, other details will be added to the description to attract candidates, such as working hours, salary, and fringe benefits.

A job description should be prepared for every position in your organization. It is not enough to say, "Everyone knows what a secretary does." What does this *particular* secretary do? The main headings on the following sample indicate the typical information included in job descriptions.

Saint Paul Church
1223 West 10th
Yreka, CA 96097

JOB DESCRIPTION

JOB TITLE: Youth Choir Director

DESCRIPTION OF WORK:
General Statement of Duties: Provides training and director-ship to three youth choirs: elementary (grades 3–5), junior high (grades 6–8), and high school (grades 9–12 by audition only); leads them in liturgical celebrations on Sundays and solemnities.
Supervision Received: Receives supervision, guidance, and liturgy planning from the director of music ministries.
Supervision Exercised: Supervises youth choirs during rehearsals and liturgies; coordinates with the accompanist.

MAJOR DUTIES:
1. Conducts weekly rehearsals for three parish choirs: elementary, junior high, and high school.
2. Coordinates music selection and liturgy planning with the director of music ministries.
3. Conducts choirs at Sunday liturgies twice a month and on specified solemnities.
4. Attends monthly staff meetings with the director of music ministries.

MINIMUM QUALIFICATIONS:
Required knowledge, skills, and abilities:
1. Must have vocal training.
2. Must be able to sight read music.
3. Must have the ability to teach children of varying age levels.
4. Must have knowledge of and experience in working with the changing voice at the junior high level.
Education: B.A. degree in Music Education or the equivalent.
Experience: Must have at least one year of experience in teaching music to children.

Fig. 14. Job description.

Employee Manuals

Large organizations often issue manuals setting forth rules and describing policies and procedures that are to be followed. What does an employee do if he or she becomes sick? To whom do they report their illness? How is an employee compensated for overtime? How is vacation and sick time to be computed? How does an employee file a grievance? What kinds of conduct are prohibited? What disciplinary action may be taken? The answers to these and other questions should be covered in an employee manual.

The needs of each organization are so difficult and manuals are so varied that it is not practical to reproduce an example. If you do not have an employee handbook or manual and believe that one would be helpful, the following ideas may guide you through some of the initial planning:

Size. While many organizations publish manuals in small, convenient-to-carry sizes, we recommend that the standard paper size of 8 1/2″ by 11″ be used. Smaller size paper is inconvenient to use, requires cutting and possibly special reproduction equipment that discourage timely changes. In addition, employees do not usually carry their manuals around, so smaller ones tend to get lost under other paperwork.

Binding. Three-hole drilled paper is recommended. A stapled booklet is difficult to change. A greater number of holes requires custom drilling—an additional expense and inconvenience—that also discourages the timely publication of changes.

Numbering for reference. Each paragraph should be numbered to provide accurate reference points. The numbering system must allow for future additions. A decimal system works very well, with major divisions of the handbook assigned whole numbers, for example:

400.00.   *Working Conditions*
400.10.   *Attendance.* Frequent or excessive lateness for work without . . .
400.11.   *Failure to call or report for work.* If an employee fails to . . .

400.20.   *Authorized absences.*
400.21.   *Holidays.* The following days are observed as
           paid holidays: New Year's Day, Presidents'
           Day, . . .
400.212.   *Compensation for work on holidays.* Employees
           who are required to work on holidays will be
           compensated . . .
400.22.   *Sick leave.* Employees . . .

Style. Simple, straightforward language is the best. Attempts to be
informal and personal may sound friendly to a new employee
but irritating to established personnel.

Computer software is now available to assist you in devising
an employee manual. It can give you a good start putting your
policies and rules on paper.

Work Records

Good personnel management requires that accurate work
records be maintained. Some organizations develop their own
forms to record attendance and employee absences. An alter-
native is to use employee timekeeping records and stock
employee rating forms, which can be found in local business
supply stores. If you are not satisfied with the way employee
work records are being maintained, see if standard forms offer
an improvement.

Personnel Evaluations

Annual or semiannual personnel evaluations are common in
business, industry, and government. They are best seen as a
tool to be used to let employees know how their performance
measures up to expectations. Properly used, they are a com-
munications tool that focuses discussion between a supervisor
and a subordinate. It is an opportunity to commend a person's
good performance and recognize an individual's strong points.
It is also an opportunity to identify any weaknesses and discuss
how they might be improved. Using a Performance Evaluation
Report form to describe a worker's overall performance brings

an objective and less personal approach to the dialogue. The "sandwich" approach that we described earlier allows the supervisor to make observations of areas needing improvement between areas of performance that are commendable.

When Personnel Evaluation Reports are the basis for pay increases and/or promotion, they take on a more threatening quality. At best, they may report only commendable performance, since a person's career is at stake. The narrative portion of these reports becomes an art form all of its own, and woe be to the person whose evaluator lacked a vocabulary filled with glowing adjectives and adverbs. At worst, a bad supervisor can use an evaluation report as a whip to dominate those who are being evaluated.

Personnel Evaluation Reports that are used to improve performance can be useful tools. Personnel Evaluation Reports that damage or, at the other extreme, boost someone's career often lead to the loss of exceptional people. We prefer to see pay and promotion issues completely separate from performance evaluations.

Stock Personnel Evaluation Reports can be found in most business office supply stores. Management consulting firms may also be able to provide a Personnel Evaluation Report package that includes instruction manuals as well as report forms. If an evaluation system is new to your organization, it may be worth the expense of hiring professionals to set one up. An orientation program for everyone and an instruction program for all evaluators is an important step in getting off on the right foot.

For the evaluation program to bring about the results you want, employees will need to view the evaluation sessions as an opportunity for "us" to see how things are going and what "we" need to do to gain the best results.

Some formal evaluation programs ask the employee and the supervisor to concentrate on a limited number of goals during the new rating period. When the evaluation period arrives, they discuss whether or not the goals were achieved. If not, they ask were the goals reasonable? This kind of evaluation requires preparation and training for both evaluator and employee. Poorly executed, it can cause more personnel problems than it solves. A simple kind of evaluation may be more appropriate for your organization, especially if you are just beginning an employee evaluation program.

Evaluating and writing evaluation reports is not an easy task. In fact, it is tempting to avoid establishing such a program, if one does not already exist. As a leader, however, you have a responsibility to encourage the best performance possible from your workers. In turn, they have a need to know how they are doing. The personnel evaluation used by a school principal for teachers may be more formal than an evaluation used by a choir director, but the principle of letting workers know how their performance stacks up applies to both.

Files

The most crucial element in managing paperwork is the ability to retrieve a particular document in a timely manner. If you have ever wasted a half hour looking through stacks of paper in your office for an item, you probably vowed that one day you would get things organized. Such frustrations are symptoms of paper management disorder.

If you are moving into a well-organized parish or office, you will likely discover that the staff has an effective filing system in place. In that case, all you will have to do is learn the system. If you are establishing a new office or parish, however, you will need to start your own system. An experienced secretary can be of great help in setting up a filing system. It is also a good idea to visit others with a similar job to see how they organize their files.

The files of a parish office will be more extensive that those of a religious education director, a music director, a volunteer coordinator, or a youth minister. But most church leaders find it necessary to maintain some kind of system to manage paperwork.

Four filing systems are commonly used in offices:

Alphabetical. File folders are arranged in alphabetical order. This filing system is the most common. It is often sufficient for simple paper management requirements.

Subject. Files are grouped according to subject matter. As a practical matter, office files are often a combination of both alphabetical and subject systems. File folders dealing with subjects would be organized alphabetically:

Annual Reports
Budget
Choir
Correspondence
Personnel
Policy
Religious Education

Numerical. Some complex systems use file numbers. File numbers are useful when an organization handles a large amount of paperwork dealing with various subjects. Social work agencies often use this kind of filing system. Here's an example of the numerical system used in a large office:

300.00.	**Choir**
310.00.	Choir Members
320.00.	Choir Music Orders
400.00.	**Correspondence**
410.00.	Diocesan
420.00.	Bishop
430.00.	Pastor
440.00.	Business
441.00.	Vendors
441.10.	Church Goods Suppliers
441.11.	Church Bulletins
442.00.	Construction

Geographical. This system is used when location is of major importance or where files are grouped by zip code for mailing. For example, church files may be organized geographically according to prayer group locations: Simmons (North), Trillo (Northeast), McQuade (South), Hartigan (Southwest).

All of these systems can be combined so that they form a filing system that meets the organization's needs.

Having a filing system does not automatically guarantee success. The staff must be united in an effort to make the system work.

When paperwork arrives in an office it must be reviewed by a responsible person who can determine what to do with it.

Does the secretary open letters addressed to the pastor? If an item is to be shared with certain members of the staff, does the secretary circulate the original or the copy while the original is filed? People who receive letters and memos must be sure that those items ultimately get filed. Written guidelines are often needed in large offices to explain what happens to paperwork once it arrives.

Fortunately, most parish operations are not large and complicated. A letter arriving from the chamber of commerce inviting the pastor to bless the fishing fleet next month will be answered by the pastor. The pastor's reply will be stapled on top of the chamber of commerce letter and placed in the correspondence file. If everyone cooperates in keeping the paper moving, it can be that simple.

How can you keep from losing important correspondence? If experience shows that the pastor tends to take correspondence home where it get buried under a heap of other pressing business, a capable secretary will see that the original stays in the office, while the pastor gets a "work" copy. The secretary can then review a "pending" file and give the pastor occasional reminders about the expected reply.

If employees remove items from the file after they have been filed, there is a danger that these items may be lost, at least temporarily. Some offices use a lined paper "sign-out" sheet showing a description of the document, the name of the person taking the item, and the date removed, which then replaces the item in the file. When the item is returned, the date is recorded. Sign-out sheets are often printed on heavy, tinted paper so that they are easily noticeable in the file.

How long should files be kept? Some church records need to be maintained as official historical documents. Official documents, such as sacramental records, are never destroyed. Other items will be of historical interest and should be kept because of their future importance. Financial reports should be filed for relatively long periods of time—some offices retain them for at least seven years. The length of time varies according to the storage capacity of the office, but many experienced office managers purge their files of routine paperwork that is more than four years old. Policy statements can be removed when they are superseded by new policy statements or when they are rescinded.

Computers have taken over the work done by typewriters in many parishes. Consequently, correspondence files can be condensed by storing written material on a floppy disc or CD-ROM. Associating the incoming paper in the parish file with the outgoing response on a computer disc means that a system of cross-referencing should be devised. A penciled notation can be entered in the corner of the incoming letter to refer to the computer file designation of the reply.

Correspondence Samples

Some types of correspondence recur with enough frequency that it is helpful to keep a master copy to consult when creating a new one. In fact, such a practice enables you to improve upon the earlier work with a minimum amount of time expended. As you look at the earlier effort that took so much time and thought, it is amazing how a better way of saying something will "jump out" at you.

Computers and electronic typewriters make it possible to send form letters that have a personal touch. All you need to do is enter the name and address, select the code for the letter you want sent, and your equipment does the rest. Other letters probably will require more work, though.

Letters of recommendation, consolation, reprimand, or congratulations often demand some reflection and revision. The ways in which you organized your thoughts and in which you expressed yourself in earlier letters will make work on the new correspondence that much easier. If you write recurring letters, keep samples in a loose-leaf notebook for ready reference.

The effective leader may not necessarily be an expert in office management, but he or she must appreciate the need to manage the paperwork associated with the position, even if it means looking for good ideas and efficient practices by other leaders. Members of your parish who work in business, industry, and government may have a wealth of sound ideas on how you can adapt their practices to your work. They would be honored to be asked.

11

Leadership for a Promising Future

A Diversity of Gifts

Most Christian denominations long for the time when differences can be laid aside and Christian unity becomes a reality. The ecumenical movement encourages us to actively seek that goal. As a consequence, we live in an age of greater openness. A new spirit of cooperation between churches can be found today in many communities where it did not exist just a few decades ago.

It is an age in which the success of one segment of Christianity should bring a sense of rejoicing to all denominations. Similarly, when one Christian group encounters difficulty, it should be a matter of concern to everyone. When part of the body suffers, the entire body becomes sick. Healing is in order.

Chapter 11 examines a serious problem in the Roman Catholic Church—the dramatic decline in vocations to the priesthood and religious life. It is so serious that Protestant military chaplains routinely visit Catholic seminaries to recruit because the few Catholic chaplains on active duty cannot be spared. The mean age of Catholic clergy continues to increase, while deaths, retirements, and departures diminish the ranks of those who are active. The number of priestless parishes increases.

Protestant readers may find that the leadership challenge in this crisis applies to their own denomination. The problems may be different, but the need for positive, effective leadership remains the same. Wherever they exist, problems need to be resolved.

The Partnership

The work of Scripture scholars, particularly in the latter part of the twentieth century, gives us new insight concerning the way God invites humankind to work with him. Following the publication of the encyclical letter *Divino Afflante Spiritu* by Pope Pius XII in 1943, scholars were encouraged to apply recent discoveries in archeology, ancient history, linguistics, and other sciences to the study of Sacred Scripture.[1] The resulting work used the tools of literary and form criticism and provided a better vision of God working through the person of the human author.[2]

When we become open to seeing God work in and through others, as in the case of biblical authors, we gain a new appreciation of how God works in the world. We see him working through those around us, and if we cooperate, he works through us. The "chance" meeting with someone who changes our life for the better may be seen as God working through another person to touch us and perhaps heal us. Seen in retrospect, life is full of many such "mystical" encounters.

With that insight, we discover that God has been inviting humankind to work with him to make the world a better place throughout the centuries. We know that it is good to pray for God's assistance, but it is important to recognize that God invites us to be a part of his plan as well. For example, while people prayed for better weather for their crops, others used their God-given intelligence and skills to build dams to control floods and provide water in dry seasons. While people prayed for a cure for polio, some used their talents to discover a means to prevent the disease. To reiterate, God invites people to work with him in making this world a better place.

As a leader in the Church, you have received that same invitation in a very special way. As a leader in your organization, you are accepting that invitation to be a partner in God's program—to be a problem solver.

In his book *The Dysfunctional Church,* Franciscan scholar, author, and preacher, Father Michael H. Crosby applies the psychology of the dysfunctional family to the Church.[3] Crosby also finds hope for a cure of dysfunctional behavior in the Gospel of Matthew. The organizational difficulties Crosby identifies in his work are serious ones. To ignore them is a form of denial.

Many problems can also be seen as evidence of a need for effective and creative leadership. In today's competitive world, leaders are expected to be problem solvers.

In a more primitive ecclesiology the Church was seen as God's work, and it was the duty of the hierarchy to safeguard it. This type of management amounts to a kind of custodial care. Custodial care involves no risk-taking. It also means that organizational problems will probably be addressed only by prayer: it's God's problem, so we'll tell him about it!

Over the centuries various ecclesiologies developed. Vatican II's *Dogmatic Constitution on the Church* depicts the Church as the "pilgrim people of God" with more emphasis placed upon the human reality of the Church. Our thesis and our experience has been that God truly works through and with ordinary human beings. Consequently, we submit that God wants church leaders at all levels to be problem solvers, not mere custodians, which means being open to the work of the Holy Spirit within others and within oneself.

We have already observed that one of the serious problems within the Roman Catholic Church today is the lack of new vocations to the priesthood. It is properly called the "vocations crisis," for it is a true crisis. Few young men in the United States seek ordination; at the same time, the mean age of the clergy moves to the "downhill" side of middle age. Various solutions have been suggested, such as a married clergy, female priests, increased sacramental faculties for permanent deacons, or short-term celibate service, but there is a reluctance to break from a 900-year tradition. As a young priest once remarked, "One thing that distinguishes the Catholic Church from other Christian denominations is that it is an Eucharistic community of believers. But what the Church is doing by insisting on a male, celibate clergy is to deny the Eucharist to people in priestless communities."

What is the answer? Management experts advise, "If organizations and societies are to make progress, . . . leaders must be able to detect when routines are becoming dysfunctional. They must be able to see when routines are smothering creative planning and blocking necessary advancement."[4]

Leaders have to make decisions they do not like. The captain of the *Titanic* certainly did not want to give the order to abandon his sinking ship on a dark, cold night on the Atlantic. But the reality of the crisis made it necessary. The vocations crisis needs to be addressed realistically as well.

Obstacles in the Roadway

As a newly-arrived executive begins to make improvements in an organization, he or she is likely to encounter an objection: "But we've always done it this way!" A warning flag should go up in the executive's mind—this employee is wearing blinders. Creative thinking has stopped. Unless the employee can be encouraged to envision new possibilities, he or she will continue to be a liability to the organization. If the organization is filled with such people, it will lack vitality and become obsolete.

Successful organizations need problem solvers who are in touch with the progress in today's society. A company that refused to respond to the development of the automobile and limited itself to the continued production of buggy whips simply set itself on a course to destruction. Your role as a leader is to keep the Church vital and strong.

• One highly respected church leader spoke of the need for a continuing discussion of the ordination of women. If discussion is closed, he said, many men and women will simply say goodbye to a Church they feel is out of touch with the world. Another highly placed church official objected. He said that the Church must not be afraid of losing members because of its position on the ordination of women. It must not be afraid, he said, to be countercultural.

Countercultural. Does that strike a familiar note? It is a variation of "But we've always done it this way," only using more sophisticated language. It is a sign of limited possibilities and limited problem-solving capacity. Such limitations prevent an organization from being all that it can be. It seriously limits its potential. It is a cause for concern because it ignores the presence of a significant problem and the means to solve it.

Limited vision caused the Church to condemn Galileo in 1633 for holding that the Earth was not the center of the universe. It took more than 350 years for church leadership to admit their mistake. "But we've always thought this way," is another variation of "But we've always done it this way," and equally debilitating to an organization.

Leaders are meant to be problem solvers. Church leaders are not alone—it is a partnership with God. The task of leaders at all levels is to make the Church as healthy and strong as possible.

"Impediment of Age"

The late Reverend William Feree, S.M., was a problem solver. Seeing the steady decline in vocations in the Roman Catholic Church, he acted to do something about it. He established a Second Career program for single men and women who had completed one career and wanted to serve God in a second career.

According to Father Feree's research, "mature" vocations were the norm for centuries within the Church. When compulsory education emerged in recent times a shift occurred toward youthful vocations. This pattern moved boys from high school to the seminary. Consequently, seminaries began to deal with younger and more immature men. Older men no longer fit into the seminary living, instructional, and formation programs. There emerged a typical excuse for not accepting older men. It was called the "impediment of age."

Because of the decline in young applicants for the priesthood and the work of Father Feree and others like him, this artificial impediment has been dropped. Today, some seminaries exist mainly for older applicants, while other seminaries have opened their doors to older men.

There is a reason, however, to consider an "impediment of age" for the other end of one's ministerial career. The Church in many instances has been slow to develop an appropriate retirement program for clergy and religious. The United States devised the Social Security program in the mid-1930s so that people would not have to work until they were too ill or passed on. Other supplementary retirement programs exist, with the result that most people expect to retire and enjoy the golden years.

The mandatory age for the retirement of bishops in the Roman Catholic Church is seventy-five. Many bishops consider this to be the minimum as well—and they expect the same of their clergy! With the decline in the priesthood, keeping each man active into old age has become almost a necessity.

But this expedient carries a heavy price. Frequently, elder clergy are operating with an obsolete ecclesiology, an outdated theology, an inadequate education in behavioral sciences, and an ineffective preaching style. While older members in the congregation may sympathize with "poor old Father," younger members are not so forgiving.

- Reverend P. J. was a "retired" member of a religious order noted for its preaching. He liked to offer his services to a large church in the southern part of the state during the busy seasons of Christmas and Easter. He was a pleasant man in the rectory and most willing to take on whatever tasks were assigned. Unfortunately, he had not bothered to learn the new Rite of Reconciliation. Further, the way he heard confessions left the schoolchildren confused—he did not use the ritual they had been taught. But the worst was yet to come. Although his order was noted for preaching, P. J. spent no time preparing homilies. Instead he used the great liturgical events of the Christian year to reprimand people for not attending church during the rest of the year. Confronted with complaints of parishioners and associate pastors alike, the pastor agreed that P. J. would no longer be invited to assist in the parish. By this time, though, the people had been subjected to Reverend P. J.'s poor liturgies for a number of years. The damage had already been done.

- Reverend S. B. was in his eighties when he was assigned to a small church in a coastal town where a large number of retirees lived. Alone and without much to do, S. B. turned to drink. He habitually arrived at Saturday evening vigil services in an intoxicated condition and had to leave the altar two or three times during the liturgy. His behavior had a marked effect upon parishioners and visitors. The situation was corrected when his religious superior was contacted, and

Reverend S. B. was treated for alcoholism. He was reassigned after treatment to a supportive religious community and replaced by a younger man.

In some parishes members call to find out who will be the presider at a given liturgy. Usually the reason for such calls is a concern about the quality of the liturgy. It is hard enough for parents to get young people to attend church functions without adding the effects of the generation gap.

In contrast to the conditions in the Church, business, industry, and government generally encourage early retirement. This policy results in a refreshing upward mobility within the organization, bringing people to leadership positions during a time of their maximum contribution to the organization. To build a strong, healthy Church there is a need for young, energetic people of creative ability to fill leadership roles in a similar fashion.

- Reverend J. E. admitted that he wanted to become a priest back in the Bing Crosby, *Going My Way* era because the young assistant pastor at the parish church was a good role model. On the other hand, he did not find the stern, older pastor to be an inspiring figure.

One should not infer from this discussion that elderly clergy as a group are not capable of serving. Outstanding examples of pastoral ministry by those over sixty-five can be found in every diocese and religious order. On the other hand, some will experience burnout before reaching that age. Those who wish to continue to serve should be considered for assignments in which their positive attributes will be fully utilized and their negative qualities minimized. There is no substitute for competency. The Reverend P. J. did very well visiting shut-ins during the Christmas and Easter seasons. On a one-to-one encounter with people, he was charming. His performance in front of a congregation, however, was damaging to the Church.

Clergy, along with others in society, should have the opportunity to enjoy the golden years. They, too, should be able to enjoy God's gift of creation without the pressure of daily duties. They've earned it. Yes, retirement programs, especially those with a decent supplementary income, can be expensive.

But there is also an incalculable cost to keeping the ineffectual in fully active assignments.

The emphasis placed on seniority has another destructive effect. It means that often a person is appointed to a very responsible position just because they have "put in their time." A person may be appointed as a pastor because everyone else ordained in his group already has been made pastor. Stories told at clergy gatherings indicate that unstable and eccentric people are nevertheless appointed to important posts. They often stay at their last assignment upon retirement—continuing to be a disruptive presence while a new pastor struggles to establish leadership.

We have painted a rather dismal picture of the present situation. What can be done to build the strong and vital Church of the future for which we long?

A Personnel Management Program

Successful organizations are built upon a wide recruiting base. The more people who apply for a position, the more selective management can be. Many applicants seek to become firefighters, police officers, pilots, flight attendants, military officers, nurses, and teachers. Administrators can set high selection standards and accept only the best qualified applicants. Some applicants will be disqualified during training. Those who receive an appointment usually enter a probationary period of a year or more or work under a temporary contract.

Successful organizations normally have in place some kind of competitive selection process for promotions. This process may involve study, examinations, interviews, or work evaluation assessment, or combinations of the above. When a member of the organization is promoted, frequently another probationary period or internship assignment occurs. Some will not complete this period satisfactorily and will return to their former position. It is not a perfect process, but it does tend to bring the best qualified people to top positions within the organization. The more promotion levels that exist within the organization, the more opportunities there will be to screen applicants for top positions.

Can this process be made to work in the Church? Specifically, can it be made to work among the clergy? Yes, it can. And the sooner the better for the health of the Church. It begins with building a wide selection base.

What about promotions among the clergy that "don't work out?" There's no probationary period for them, is there? A pastor who lacks the skills necessary for a position can be returned to his previous position. The biggest difficulty is discovering that an individual is not suited to be a pastor. Some form of performance evaluation is necessary. Superiors need to know how their subordinates are performing.

Promotion to bishop is unique, for it is accompanied by a permanent sacramental action that cannot be dissolved if the bishop lacks the skills necessary for the position. Nevertheless, there is no reason why a mistake in the selection process should continue to haunt the faithful. A bishop who lacks the proper leadership skills can still handle the many ceremonial functions of a busy diocese while another bishop skilled in administration and personnel management can devote energy to running the diocese effectively. In other words, even a bishop can be assigned with the idea of maximizing personal strengths while minimizing personal weaknesses.

However, attention needs to be given to a selection process that will minimize mistakes in promotions. For centuries the Church has been obsessed with the fear of heresy and a concomitant obsession with orthodoxy. As a result, the selection process has been more concerned with, "Does he think like I do?" rather than, "Is he an effective leader?" In this age of ecumenism the fear of various ideas seems to be a bit irrational, particularly since we recognize that God may speak to us through others who do not think precisely as we do. If someone is being selected for a position of leadership within the Church, that person's leadership ability should be the focus of attention.

The first step in building a healthy Church for the future will be to drastically increase the selection base of applicants for the clergy. Then the very best applicants can be selected in sufficient numbers to effectively minister to the faithful. This procedure demands a thoughtful strategy. It must begin with the difficult decision to change the barriers that prevent excellent candidates from consideration. It means opening the gates that have been closed. It means discarding a 900-year-old tradition that has become dysfunctional. Which of the proposed solutions should be acted upon? Perhaps, all of them?

It must also begin with making the job of the clergy attractive. It is true that the great men and women of the Church often lived in meager circumstances and often practiced various forms of self-denial. While spartan conditions may have inspired many people in past decades, it does not attract applicants today. It is not that people shun hard or even dangerous work. Look at the large number of firefighter and police applicants in a society that has grown increasingly complex and violent.

In another time, when few people even attained as much as a high school diploma, the clergy were considered among the best educated members of society, which gave them a sense of satisfaction. Today we live in a society where many people are better educated than most clergy. A sense of being part of an "elite" vocation highly admired by the people is now gone.

What can make the clergy attractive today?

The job itself carries with it the true joy of doing the Lord's work; a sense of that special "partnership." But that alone is not sufficient.

Working and living conditions need to be reasonable, which means working hours that provide some private time. As an experienced pastor said, "There are three periods during the day that one can work: morning, afternoon, and evening. If you work all three, you'll burn yourself out." Middle-of-the-night emergency calls serve as a reminder that clergy are never completely off-duty. Firefighters often have a work shift of being on-duty for twenty-four hours and off-duty for forty-eight hours. In most businesses, a forty-hour work week is standard. The vast majority of employees work five eight-hour days a week with two days off, but some businesses have experimented with four ten-hour days a week with three days off. The point is that when clergy are expected to work from 6 a.m. until 11 p.m. six or seven days a week, the demand is far too different from the rest of society. Such a demanding schedule makes the job unattractive. It also creates clergy burnout.

Vacation time needs to be adequate as well and should also compare favorably with the vacation policy of other organizations. Ministers who are unable to pry themselves away from their work ultimately reduce their effectiveness and impair their health.

- Pastor P. M. was allowed a four-week vacation each year, but he would only take one week and usually remained in the rectory. He continued to attend meetings and accept telephone calls during this week. As a consequence, he remained buried in his work and lacked the fresh vision and renewed energy that a real vacation can offer.

The work space should be as professional and attractive as possible. An office need not be luxurious, but it should be a comfortable place to work and confer with others. Working out of a room originally intended to be a storage closet without windows or ventilation or sharing an office may be an operational necessity at times, but it will not attract others to the profession.

For clergy who live in a church-provided rectory, the living quarters must be clean, comfortable, and suitably furnished. Meals should be wholesome, balanced, and tastefully prepared. If more than one person lives in the house, the pastor or superior has a clear leadership responsibility to provide this service for others. Married clergy will usually have an advantage in their living conditions. A rectory is a poor substitute for home life! In any event, if we want to attract others to the profession, living conditions must be healthy and comfortable.

- One diocese established a policy that only clergy who live alone could have pets. This policy prevented many undesirable living conditions that can often result when members of a group living together inflict their pets on others.

Compensation must be adequate. In many cases it is not. It is unfortunate that clergy must depend on stipends and gifts from the congregation to pay for their vacations. It is an archaic practice that is inappropriate for professionals in today's world. A salary should also allow one to have enough money to establish savings and to provide for a retirement supplement. Medical and dental insurance should be part of the compensation package as well. In some parts of the United States, cars are provided for the clergy; in other areas, they are not, but an additional allowance is provided for that purpose. If an automobile is provided, it should be in good condition, not a junker. A junker implies that poor equipment is the best that the Church can offer. An adequate salary is also of special concern to married clergy who have family expenses to consider. If we are to attract competent people, compensation must be within a range that will allow a respectable standard of living. Admittedly, it costs money to attract and retain good people, but we lose money when we do not have such people serving in our organization.

A realistic retirement program should allow clergy to plan for the future. Longer life expectancy allows most of our citizens to dream of a time when they will be able to rest from their labors and rejoice in the Lord's gift. Other people look forward to time spent fishing, writing, painting, traveling, or discovering new hobbies in their retirement. It should be no different for clergy. A realistic retirement age combined with a living plan for retirees should give a prospective candidate an idea of what the future may hold. Government service leads the way by making a retirement package part of their recruiting program, but it can be a part of clergy recruitment, too. People seeking ordination should have a vision of the time when their active service will likely end and know what provisions will be made for them.

Assuming that greatly increased numbers of people enter the ministry, seminary facilities would be stretched beyond their present capacities. What can be done to accelerate the Master of Divinity program leading to ordination? Does the curriculum need revision? Does it need to focus more on preparing clergy for what they actually do? Can new instructional techniques such as self-paced learning be used to accelerate and improve the learning process? Finally, can some classes be presented as workshops in communities outside the seminary? If a significant increase in applicants is our goal, then we must be prepared to deal with these numbers in an efficient, time-sensitive way in seminary programs. Such changes will require bold leadership and creative thinking.

Looking toward the Future

In the healthy, vital Church of the future, the increased number of energetic, available clergy will have the immediate effect of improving the quality of ministry within the Church. Priestless parishes will have clergy, overworked pastors will gain associates, and the workload will reach more reasonable levels. As the newly ordained gain more experience and become available for promotion to pastor, the selection base will be large enough to allow for the advancement of the best qualified personnel.

In the healthy, vital Church of the future, sexual and psychological breakdowns among the clergy that detract from the Church's standing will be reduced. A larger number of applicants would allow for a tighter screening process. If married clergy are allowed as part of the vocation crisis solution, the benefit of a healthy sexuality will be brought to the ministry.

In the healthy, vital Church of the future, the greater numbers of clergy will make continuing education programs more available, since those in advanced studies will not leave unfilled vacancies in a parish. These vacancies will be able to be filled.

In the healthy, vital Church of the future, the upward mobility of younger clergy will allow promotions to the higher levels of the Church to be made from an ever larger pool of better qualified people.

In the healthy, vital Church of the future, parents will be more supportive of their children to enter church service and seek ordination.

Most important, in the healthy, vital Church of the future, people will draw greater inspiration from their clergy. They will worship with increased fervor, act with religious conviction, and seek to draw closer to their God. The Church is always the Pilgrim People of God. The people can be strengthened for their journey by bringing effective leadership to bear on the vocation crisis. Real leaders are problem solvers.

That is such an important statement that we will say it again, this time with more emphasis. Real leaders are problem solvers!

Notes

Chapter 1: Leadership—The Person

1. Max DePree, *Leadership Is an Art* (New York: Dell Publishing, 1989), 1.

2. James M. Kouzes and Barry Z. Posner, *The Leadership Challenge* (San Francisco: Jossey-Bass Publishers, 1987), 15.

3. Peter F. Drucker, *The Effective Executive* (New York: HarperCollins Publishers, 1985), 23.

4. H. Jackson Brown, Jr., *Life's Little Instruction Book* (Nashville: Rutledge Hill Press, 1991), n. 190.

5. Kouzes and Posner, *Leadership Challenge,* 155.

6. Dale Carnegie, *How to Win Friends and Influence People,* rev. ed. by Donna Carnegie and Dorothy Carnegie (New York: Simon and Schuster, 1982), 24.

7. Kouzes and Posner, *Leadership Challenge,* 21.

8. Ibid., 11.

9. William G. Saltonstall, "Where Do You Stand?," *This Week Magazine,* May 14, 1961, 2.

10. Drucker, *Effective Executive,* 143.

11. Carnegie, *How to Win Friends,* 25.

12. Kouzes and Posner, *Leadership Challenge,* 180.

13. Carnegie, *How to Win Friends,* 205–49.

14. Max DePree, *Leadership Jazz* (New York: Doubleday, 1992), 32.

15. John Powell, S.J., *Unconditional Love* (Allen, Tex.: Argus, 1978), 63–64.

Chapter 2: The Approach to Leadership

1. Max DePree, *Leadership Is an Art* (New York: Dell Publishing, 1989), 101.

2. James M. Kouzes and Barry Z. Posner, *The Leadership Challenge* (San Francisco: Jossey-Bass Publishers, 1987), 164.

3. Mike Schmoker, "The Deming Way," *The Sunday Oregonian,* January 26, 1992, B7–10.

4. George S. Odiorne, *Management Decisions by Objectives* (Englewood Cliffs, N.J.: Prentice-Hall, 1969), 3.

5. Robert J. Kriegel and Louis Patler, *If It Ain't Broke . . . BREAK IT!* (New York: Warner Books, 1991), 159.

6. George S. Patton, Jr., *War as I Knew It* (Boston: Houghton Mifflin, 1947), 354.

Chapter 3: Rules of the Leadership Game

1. Lester R. Bittel, *What Every Supervisor Should Know* (New York: McGraw-Hill, 1959), 75.

2. Ibid., 73.

3. Max DePree, *Leadership Is an Art* (New York: Dell Publishing, 1989), 19.

4. Department of the Army, "Morale," *Military Leadership, Psychology, and Personnel Management* (Army Field Forces: U.S. Army, 1948), 599–602.

Chapter 4: The Business of Leadership

1. A. C. Germann, *Police Executive Development* (Springfield, Ill.: Charles C. Thomas, Publisher, 1962), 50. Dr. Germann credits an earlier work by Luther Gulick for the widely used mnemonic POSDCORB (Planning, Organizing, Staffing, Directing, Coordinating, Reporting, and Budgeting) that we adapt here, in part, for our understanding of church leadership. We have added Counseling, Instructing, and Evaluating, which have emerged as essential functions as well. Gulick's work appeared in "Notes on the Theory of Organization," Luther Gulick and L. Urwick, eds., *Papers on the Science of Administration* (New York: Institute of Public Administration, 1937), 13.

2. Peter F. Drucker, *Managing for the Future* (New York: Truman Talley Books/Dutton, 1992), 121–22.

3. Max DePree, *Leadership Is an Art* (New York: Dell Publishing, 1989), 9.

4. H. Norman Schwarzkopf and Peter Petre, *It Doesn't Take a Hero* (New York: Bantam Books, 1993), 77.

Chapter 5: A Few Words on Supervision

1. George S. Patton, Jr., *War as I Knew It* (Boston: Houghton Mifflin, 1947), 354, 401.

2. Adapted from Lester R. Bittel, *What Every Supervisor Should Know* (New York: McGraw-Hill, 1959), 5.

3. Ibid., 59.

4. "Staff officers of inharmonious disposition, irrespective of their ability, must be removed. A staff cannot function properly unless it is a united family." See Patton, *War as I Knew It,* 361.

Chapter 6: Managing for Results

1. Peter F. Drucker, *Managing for the Future* (New York: Truman Talley Books/Dutton, 1992), 221.

2. Adapted from "How to Make the Most of Your Time," *U.S. News and World Report,* December 3, 1973, 46.

3. Peter F. Drucker, *The Effective Executive* (New York: HarperCollins Publishers, 1985), 27.

4. R. Alec Mackenzie, *The Time Trap* (New York: American Management Association, 1972), 20–29.

5. Drucker, *Effective Executive,* 49.

6. Mackenzie, *Time Trap,* 22.

7. Ibid., 29, 93–96.

8. Ibid., 10.

9. Ibid., 87–92.

10. Ibid., 98–112.

11. Ibid., 36.

12. Ibid., 70.

13. Drucker, *Effective Executive,* 38.

14. Mackenzie, *Time Trap,* 49–53.

15. Frank A. Nunlist, "Wanted: Executive Time Power," *Dun's Review,* October 1967, as cited by Mackenzie, *Time Trap,* 55.

16. Mackenzie, *Time Trap,* 117.

17. Ibid., 56.

18. Manuel J. Smith, *When I Say No, I Feel Guilty* (New York: Bantam Books, 1975), 30–31.

19. Ibid., 74–75.

20. George S. Odiorne, *Management Decisions by Objectives* (Englewood Cliffs, N.J.: Prentice-Hall, 1969), 8.

21. Ibid., 25.

22. Robert F. Mager, *Goal Analysis* (Belmont, Calif.: Lake Publishing Co., 1984), 40.

23. Peter F. Drucker, *Managing for the Future,* 121.

Chapter 7: Organizing the Organization

1. Material in this chapter is based on student study material prepared by the author, "Organizational Chart Construction," Portland State University, 1970, and "Organizational Structure— Charts and Chart Construction," a training publication by the Traffic Institute, Northwestern University, Evanston, Ill., 1960.

Chapter 9: Let's Have a Meeting!

1. James M. Kouzes and Barry Z. Posner, *The Leadership Challenge* (San Francisco: Jossey-Bass Publishers, 1987), 270.

2. R. Alec Mackenzie, *The Time Trap* (New York: American Management Association, 1972), 108.

3. Much of the material in the following sections has been adapted from *24 Group Methods and Techniques in Adult Education* produced and published by Educational Systems Corp., Washington, D.C., with funds provided from the United States Office of Economic Opportunity and reprinted by the Federal Bureau of Investigation, United States Depatrment of Justice, 1972.

Chapter 10: Teaching Tips for Non-Teachers

1. Robert F. Mager, *Preparing Instructional Objectives* (Belmont, Calif.: Lake Publishing Co., 1984), 5.

2. Ibid., 6.

3. For additional information on learner-centered instruction see Frank Hoffman, *How to Teach Grown-ups* (Canoga Park, Calif.: Practical Management Associates, 1979), an eight workbook/ audiocassette course. This instructional package is ideally suited for self-paced instruction in the parish setting.

Chapter 11: Leadership for a Promising Future

1. See Gerhard Lohfink, *The Gospels: God's Word in Human Words,* trans. William R. Poehlmann (Chicago: Franciscan Herald Press, 1972), for a discussion of the human effect upon Sacred Scripture.

2. Form criticism is a method of investigating the origins, growth, and evolution of elements of oral tradition about Jesus—pronouncement and miracle stories, sayings and parables, tales about Jesus, and passion narratives—that underlie the Gospels. Each form served not only a specific purpose and offered a greater understanding of the early church but also helped to resolve apparent contradictions in the Gospels.

3. Michael H. Crosby, *The Dysfunctional Church* (Notre Dame, Ind.: Ave Maria Press, 1991).

4. James M. Kouzes and Barry Z. Posner, *The Leadership Challenge* (San Francisco: Jossey-Bass Publishers, 1987), 49.

Bibliography

Bittel, Lester R. *What Every Supervisor Should Know.* New York: McGraw-Hill, 1959.

Brown, H. Jackson, Jr. *Life's Little Instruction Book.* Nashville: Rutledge Hill Press, 1991.

Carnegie, Dale. *How to Win Friends and Influence People.* Rev. ed. by Donna Carnegie and Dorothy Carnegie. New York: Simon and Schuster, 1982.

Crosby, Michael H. *The Dysfunctional Church.* Notre Dame, Ind.: Ave Maria Press, 1991.

Department of the Army. *"Morale."* In *Military Leadership, Psychology, and Personnel Management.* Army Field Forces: U.S. Army, 1948.

DePree, Max. *Leadership Is an Art.* New York: Dell Publishing, 1989.

————. *Leadership Jazz.* New York: Doubleday, 1992.

Drucker, Peter F. *The Effective Executive.* New York: HarperCollins Publishers, 1985.

————. *Managing for the Future.* New York: Truman Talley Books/ Dutton, 1992.

Germann, A. C. *Police Executive Development.* Springfield, Ill.: Charles C. Thomas, Publisher, 1962.

Gulick, Luther. "Notes on the Theory of Organization." Luther Gulick and L. Urwick, eds. *Papers on the Science of Administration.* New York: Institute of Public Administration, 1937.

Hoffman, Frank. *How to Teach Grown-ups.* Canoga Park, Calif.: Practical Management Associates, 1979.

Kouzes, James M., and Barry Z. Posner. *The Leadership Challenge.* San Francisco: Jossey-Bass Publishers, 1987.

Kriegel, Robert J., and Louis Patler. *If It Ain't Broke . . . BREAK IT!* New York: Warner Books, 1991.

Lohfink, Gerhard. *The Gospels: God's Word in Human Words.* Trans. William R. Poehlmann. Chicago: Franciscan Herald Press, 1972.

Mackenzie, R. Alec. *The Time Trap.* New York: American Management Association, 1972.

Mager, Robert F. *Goal Analysis.* Belmont, Calif.: Lake Publishing Co., 1984.

———. *Preparing Instructional Objectives.* Belmont, Calif.: Lake Publishing Co., 1984.

Nunlist, Frank A. "Wanted: Executive Time Power." *Dun's Review,* October 1967.

Odiorne, George S. *Management Decisions by Objectives.* Englewood Cliffs, N.J.: Prentice-Hall, 1969.

Pagonis, William G., with Jeffrey L. Cruikshank. *Moving Mountains.* Boston: Harvard Business School Press, 1992.

Patton, George S., Jr. *War as I Knew It.* Boston: Houghton Mifflin, 1947.

Peck, M. Scott. *A World Waiting to Be Born.* New York: Bantam Books, 1993.

Powell, John, S.J. *Unconditional Love.* Allen, Tex.: Argus, 1978.

Saltonstall, William G. "Where Do You Stand?" *This Week Magazine,* May 14, 1961.

Schmoker, Mike. "The Deming Way." *The Sunday Oregonian,* January 26, 1992.

Schwarzkopf, H. Norman, and Peter Petre. *It Doesn't Take a Hero.* New York: Bantam Books, 1993.

Smith, Manuel J. *When I Say No, I Feel Guilty.* New York: Bantam Books, 1975.

Index